NAVIGATING THE DEEP RIVER

NAVIGATING THE DEEP RIVER

Spirituality

in African

American

Families

My Sister Cheryl Elliot

ARCHIE SMITH JR.

Archie Smith, Jr.

United Church Press

Cleveland, Ohio

United Church Press, Cleveland, Ohio 44115

© 1997 by Archie Smith Jr.

Library of Congress Cataloging-in-Publication Data
Smith, Archie, 1939–
    Navigating the deep river : spirituality in African American families / Archie Smith, Jr.
        p.   cm.
    Includes bibliographical references and index.
    ISBN 0-8298-1218-0 (pbk. : alk. paper)
    1. Afro-American families—Religious life.   2. Afro-Americans—Religion. 3. Church work with Afro-American families.   I. Title.
BR563.N4S565   1997
305.896'073—dc21   97-33158
                                                                    CIP

~

To my family—my mother, Beatrice Skipper Smith,
Marji Smith Cottom, Amos Leonard Smith, Joyce Smith Long,
Geri Smith, and Geraldine Messina Smith—and to the
memory of my father, Archie Smith Sr.

CONTENTS

~

~

It is exciting to recognize a book that makes a significant contribution to one of the most important issues facing Western societies today, a book that tackles many of the interfaces of the experience of racism in mind and society. Professor Smith's book addresses itself to the structures of racism that operate as both external and internal discourses in daily life. As we move toward a new millennium, he argues that these structures can be found firmly in place in United States society, organizing the lives of African Americans in detrimental ways.

> And as the conditions of life worsen materially and spiritually within the context of postmodernism, it does not seem surprising that underclass black people feel more acutely this contemporary anguish and despair. I do not think it useful to simply name this nihilism and let it go at that, to be passively terrorized by it, we have to think and talk about the ways we critically intervene, to provide hope to offer strategies of transformation."[1]

This book on working with families within the traditions of black spirituality is one of Professor Smith's critical interventions into contemporary anguish and despair. He argues that the traditions of spirituality that are a fundamental part of the history and experience of African Americans offer a way to combat the influence of racist ideas and their paralyzing effect on the mind. Bringing these traditions into consciousness as part of therapeutic discourse offers to counselors and therapists a resource that should form a part of their therapeutic consciousness and daily practice.

Such ideas form a counterconsciouness to the postmodernist fragmented moralizing and theorizing that characterize much public discourse about black families. As black writers and therapists in both the United States and the United Kingdom have told us, the inner structures of black men and women have to accommodate these external negative images of blackness, and black people must form their identities in relation to a dominant white culture. Often their own images of themselves are devalued. Moreover, to embrace this spiritual tradition contributes a different stream to the larger American discourse in which spirituality is often marginalized in the service of economic values:

> Therapists . . . are challenged to continually examine their beliefs, and work for the transformation of the social mainstream in which they and their counselees live, move, and have their being.

Why has Archie Smith Jr. asked me to write the foreword to his book? Since I am a white, middle-class female academic and family therapist based in the United Kingdom, it could be argued that it is none of my business to comment on a book written by a black academic theologian based in the United States. However, it is not irrelevant that Archie Smith came to this country on the occasion when he wanted space to think; and it is possible that part of the context for developing the ideas in this book came from the opportunity to be freed from one particular ecostructure with its own legacy of racist experience and enter another where the experience was, for him, less predetermined. The freedom from one context and the opportunity to discuss, compare, and contrast in a white society where both racist experience and ongoing debate about how it can be combated is happening all the time triggers new freedoms of mind. In ongoing discussions with Archie Smith and readings of the texts, I have been excited by seeing this book emerge from the many strands of experience, scholarly thought, and a deeply informed theological mind, and have been proud to be myself informed by the process of the tributaries coming together into their own deep river flow.

What then is new in the book for me and how will it excite other readers in the field of social welfare, mental health practice, and psychotherapy? Since I cannot speak for those with a theological background, I will have to imagine what might be new or interesting to them.

First this is both an angry book and a profoundly hopeful book. The hope is not facile but based in a strong ecostructural analysis of the dilemmas facing black people today. Rather than subordinating the dialogue of black people to the oppressive discourses of white society, Archie Smith proposes a revision in the placing of spiritual dialogue, to regard it as one of the dominant discourses forming part of all healing processes, rather than an exotic extra for therapists and counselors to have as a tagged-on part of their repertoire. He suggests a move toward influencing the mainstream by bringing this important part of black heritage more centrally into all key public debates about human relations in the United States today. Since black people form 12 percent of U.S. society, to make this important contribution a central part of the dialogues of both black and white peoples is to make visible what is currently invisible or marginalized. By making such a discourse central, black spiritual thought and tradition would be gaining an equal voice alongside other voices, "a common belief in the parenthood of God and the kinship of all people." Whereas to deny such a voice is an impoverishment to black people, and it may also be an impoverishment to their white fellow citizens.

Secondly, the book pays powerful tribute to the development of black history, its traditions, its legacies, and the powerful beliefs that have traveled across both continents and time. The effects of racist experience on black people across the world, and the vital importance of an interactive reading of black history by and with white people, contextualize the arguments of the book in a wider arena that makes it of significant importance to readers everywhere.

Thirdly, this is a spiritual book. I challenge any reader not to be personally transformed in some aspect of their work or thinking as they move through it. This emerges from Archie Smith's concept of therapy "informed by a black church spiritual tradition that views personal and social transformation as interrelated in the reality of God. The well-being of the individual is interwoven with the well-being of the whole community."

Fourthly, the systemic approach to counseling and therapeutic treatment is very clearly developed, with a particular emphasis on looking at all the levels of context that may be affecting an individual's life. The practical and the spiritual are closely linked at this point. Archie Smith addresses himself to the questions: What is required to train caregivers to critically intervene, provide hope, and offer strategies of transformation with isolated, marginalized, or displaced exilic people? How can certain principles be developed in the field of family therapy to *enhance* the church's ministry with African American families in the context of the wider society? How can the culture of black churches, and its manner of reaching out to despairing souls, inform the work of family therapists? How can caregivers learn to positively access spiritual resources within the life of the family?"

These questions are of great importance to counselors and healers of all ethnicities on both sides of the Atlantic. Since all white people have participated in the collective history of colonization, all that we may try to do in the name of therapy may be poisoned by being a further extension of the colonizing position, unless we take relevant dimensions of the human experience and beliefs of others into account in our own thinking. "Where therapy is practiced ignorant of the whole American past, it may be impossible to detect how present-day therapeutic practices suppress awareness of African American strengths and promote Eurocentric values as the preferred or superior standard for mental and spiritual well-being. Where the objective of therapy is the adjustment of African Americans within the definitions and power arrangements of the dominant society, then it may be impossible to recognize black history and the history of other colonized groups as providing radically different and alternative views for mental health and social transformation."

Archie Smith, alongside other black thinkers in the therapeutic field, argues that both the minds and the theorizing of therapists and counselors trained in Eurocentric perspectives have to change to be of use to a black client's process of change. Such change involves the loss of familiar theories of mind, and therefore loss of power. Such loss may well relate to aspects of the ministry and to theological constructions as well as to therapeutic ones. This book offers a powerful contribution to those processes of change.

Gill Gorell Barnes
Senior Social Worker
Tavistock Clinic for Human Relations
London, England

ACKNOWLEDGMENTS

~

I am indebted to the administration, faculty, and members of the board of trustees of the Pacific School of Religion for granting me a semester's sabbatical leave to complete this manuscript. In addition, many kind souls stepped into the river of struggle and helped to clarify my thinking or offered encouragement as the manuscript developed. I could never pay the debt I owe to them. They must be acknowledged: H. Leslie Steeves, Jane Morlet Hardie, Carol Elizabeth McMillan, Mary Donovan Turner, Randi Jones Walker, Mary Ann Tolbert, Charles McCoy, Vincent Harding, Gill Gorell Barnes, John Byng-Hall, Carol Manahan, Margaret Walker, Yvette Flores Ortiz, Richard Maisel, Michael Searle, Suzanne Pregerson, Jennifer Freeman, Dean Lobovits, Andrea Aidells, Alice Sawyerr, Ann Stevens, Nurun Islam, Yvonne Jackson Browne, Audrey Englert, Nimisha Patel, Folarin Shogbamimu, Elisabeth Heismann, Chip Chimera, I. Britt Krause, Marji H. Smith Cottom, Norman Gottwald, Carroll Weaver Sadaki, Larry Kent Graham, Ursula Pfafflin, James Wm. McClendon, Karlyn Johnson Ward, Edward Sampson, Ogretta McNeil, and Marya Marthas. Gratitude extends to my clinical colleagues and staff at the Marlborough Family Service in London, England.

INTRODUCTION

In the early days, churches often helped hide slaves who were trying to escape to freedom. Members of the church would risk their lives to help these people. The church has always been a part of helping others.

Rosa Parks, *Quiet Strength*

What appears to be different today from past decades and centuries is what gives every indication of being the permanent entrapment of significant numbers of Americans, especially urban Blacks, in a world apart at the bottom of society.

Timothy J. McNully, *The Chicago Tribune*, 1985

If any of you put a stumbling block before one of these little ones who believe in me, it would be better for you if a great millstone were fastened around your neck and you were drowned in the depth of the sea.

Matthew 18:6

We must remain strong. Violence and crime seem so much more prevalent. It is easy to say that we have come a long way, but we still have a long way to go. Many of our children are going astray. But I still remain hopeful.

Rosa Parks, *Quiet Strength*

The River Metaphor: An Ecological Perspective

This book is about remaining hopeful. The river is the central metaphor. The river metaphor is well established in African American spiritual experience as expressed in the Negro spirituals "Deep River," "Roll, Jordan, Roll," and "Wade in the Waters." In this book it is used to describe the mainstream of American society and the spiritual resources of African American families. I argue that the historical context is a resource to be tapped, and that learning to tap the cultural heritage, spiritual beliefs, and metaphors that underlie family struggles is essential to effective therapy with African Americans. Three key resources will be emphasized. They are dimension of depth, or the capacity to develop depth of meaning; reflexivity; and sense of agency.

The following influences inspired the writing of this book. First is the early influences of my family of origin and my lifelong participation in African American religious communities, where I share Rosa Parks's hope (which is the hope of thousands of others). Second is a special series on African Americans that was published in the *Chicago Tribune* in 1985, entitled "The American Millstone." It graphically epitomized the plight of many African Americans and families trapped in urban centers of this wealthy democratic society. The *Chicago Tribune's* message about a new class of marginalized people, mostly black, taking root in America's inner cities and dwelling in enclaves of despair, continues to stir me. Were these images of the past, or are they images of the future? Third, the writing of this book was prompted by colleagues who frame the question of race in personal terms. They claim to be color-blind or to see black people only as unique individuals. They tend to ignore historical influences and underestimate the long-term impact of racism up black experience and on American society. They often fail to recognize a common black culture, a heritage with many rich traditions, and spirituality as a resource to be tapped. The forth influence comes from my work over the past three decades as a pastoral family therapist with African Americans and families from other cultures.

Although these influences inspire the writing of this book, it is difficult to write a book on African American families in a changing and multicultural society as complex and geographically diverse as the United States. How can one writer possibly get it right? I do not try to offer a unique perception of the issues. Instead, I offer my socially conditioned standpoint, which has been enriched by the experiences of working over time with families in the United States and the United Kingdom. I struggle with the questions that continue to emerge and demand attention. How do we find the strength to continue the struggle to remove the stumbling blocks of racism and poverty, remain strong and hopeful, and work for wider justice? This book will address this question. The aim of the book is to demonstrate how pastors and social workers can help tap the spiritual resources of African American families in order to counter a deepening sense of despair, to provide hope, and to offer strategies for transformation.

In 1980 a black theologian, J. Deotis Roberts, argued that in the black tradition the family and the church hold the key to the survival and well-being of black people. Religious institutions such as black churches represent the spiritual resources of black communities. The family represents the generativity of those resources. Together they represent culture and historical memory, an expanded sense of community, continuity, creativity, renewal, and hope in the future.

The 1980s seem far away. We are now living at the start of a new millennium, and Roberts's words are even more important now than when they were first written. Families, and especially African American families in the United States, face economic hardship, a lost sense of tradition and commitment, weakened ties to black culture, community, and institutions. They face new levels of stress, and an increase in domestic and systemic violence. As employment opportunities diminish and social services such as health care are cut or streamlined, more women, children, and men join the ranks of the homeless. In addition, those who offer family support, the caregivers, themselves are stressed or burned-out. Some caregivers believe they face insurmountable odds and cannot envision solutions from within the framework of their discipline. Other help givers come to believe that even money cannot help.

An Ecological Approach

Edgar H. Auerswald, a psychiatrist, anticipated the problem of burnout and despair in the 1960s. He recognized that with the proliferation of social problems such as unemployment, poverty and crime, personal problems increase and become more complex. The proliferation of such problems can be overwhelming for the help giver and lead to burnout. An alternative must be found.

Auerswald believed that it is impossible to adequately address or solve complex social and personal problems within the framework of a single discipline. One strategy to combat the proliferation of social problems has been an interdisciplinary approach. Here specialists pool their knowledge and share information across disciplinary boundaries. The potential benefits are that new information can come to light and greater cooperation between professionals is possible. The drawback is the strong tendency among specialists to stay within the parameters of their original training, and to defend the borders of their discipline and professional identity. The result is that information from other disciplines is treated as peripheral to the investigation at hand; "only those concepts which pose no serious challenges or language difficulties are welcomed."[1]

Auerswald offers an alternative, which he calls an ecological approach. He describes this approach as a systems orientation that encourages a professional to become a navigator or an explorer. An explorer is one who travels into uninvestigated or uncharted areas in order to learn, make new connections, and generate new information. The explorer follows the development of a problem in order to understand its emergence within a wide context. This ecological approach proceeds by focusing on the way events are organized over time and the nature of the transactions taking place around a particular event or person(s). It aims to identify the various influences that foster or hinder the growth of persons and their networks. (A network is the ensemble of family, friends, and neighbors who actively support, inspire, and sometimes restrain the individual.[2]) The strengthening of relationship networks can help counter stress and a deepening of despair. With an ecological or network focus it is possible to identify various levels of a complex situation, appreciate the interplay of forces that maintain particular difficulties, and decide what ought to be the strategies and purpose of therapeutic activity.

This approach "makes it possible to determine with much more clarity in what life arena the individual, the family, or a group of individuals needs assistance, and thus to more effectively combat the anomie and dehumanization characteristic of our age."[3] Strategies for therapeutic intervention will be developed in collaboration with the people and institutions that relate to the problem at hand. The context for therapeutic intervention, then, is much larger than the therapy room and the home. It includes the interaction of people within their environment, i.e., their network, neighborhood, hospitals, schools, courts, labor organizations, and religious and welfare institutions.

An Ecological Approach with African American Families

This ecological approach is an advance over views that consider the individual apart from a wider social context. It opens the door for workers to investigate areas that are not commonly considered to be within the framework of their discipline. Work with African Americans necessitates an ecological approach, one that takes seriously American history, democracy, racism, the environment, and black experience within a multicultural context.

If in black tradition the family and church held the key to the survival of black culture and the well-being of black people in the past, then how are they to do so now and in the future? In other words, the context in which we live makes it imperative that we listen to and take seriously what Roberts advocated in 1980 about the importance of church and family working together. This is the case because African American families are among the first to experience the impact and trauma of economic loss, social-structural change, and cutbacks in health and mental care services.

This book explores how the deepening of spiritual resources in both church and family can be part of an ecological approach and play a crucial role in therapy with African Americans. Here, the term "church" stands not only for Christian churches but also for broader expressions of the community's spiritual resources. A diversity of spiritual resources can help provide interpretive bridges between the complex workings of a larger social system, community of care, personal troubles, and a preferred future.

It is essential that the therapist or pastoral caregiver include awareness of spiritual resources in an ecological approach with African Americans. The African American church stands in a tradition that acknowledges a dialectical relationship between past, present, and future; between despair and hope; and between individuals and the larger systems within which they live. The African American church shares with the world's great faiths a belief in transcendent values and the interconnection of the material and spiritual. Religious faith and a belief in transcendent values grounds such principles as mutual respect, love, care for others and for creation. African American religious traditions find expression in prayer, song, spiritual practices, biblical faith, and social activism. Biblical faith and the appropriation of spiritual resources are at the heart of black church religion and traditions. Rosa Parks spoke for many of us when she said, "The church was and is the foundation of our community. It became our strength, our refuge, and our haven. We would pray, sing, and meet in church. We would use Scriptures, testimonies, and hymns to strengthen us against all the hatred and violence going on around us."[4] The church community has also been the foundation of the African American family. This community imparts strength, refuge, and faith. Strengthened and hope-filled families, in their turn, reach out to the wider community, help stem rising tides of despair, and deepen their faith by living it. With a deep faith in the Supreme Being, or God, the prophets of Israel, for example, consistently made the connection between rich and poor, the plight of the orphan and widow, and the larger system of social injustice and the righteousness of God (Isaiah 58:6, 8). In making these connections they were engaged in ecological thinking. The African American church community, like ancient Israel, was made aware that larger social forces have consequences for families, personal life, and the life of the soul.

It is necessary for family therapists who are not trained in biblical faith or theology to see that such a religious tradition can be a valuable resource in their own work with African American families. African American families are besieged by such personal and structural problems as racism, poverty, rape and other forms of violent crime, AIDS, and early death. Many struggle with the disease of alcoholism, the abuse of other substances, and varieties of addictions. Many live in communities that are isolated from transportation and social services, health care, and mental health resources. Even those who appear to have made it are not free from racism and various forms of discrimination. According to a 1993 *Newsweek* survey, many so-called middle-class and upper-class black professionals are "seething with grievances: over the petty indignities they still endure, the false fronts they have to put up to 'make it' in white institutions, the ways in which they're pigeonholed in 'black jobs.'"[5] Cain Hope Felder, a black biblical scholar, reflecting on this problem, wrote: "Now that we are near the end of this century, it is woefully apparent that white racism is, at least for African Americans, the most pervasive problem. For many of us, it remains not only unresolved but is often quite subtle, thus all the more pernicious."[6] Issues of self-worth that affect low-income African Americans also affect those who have "made it." Because they are perceived to have "made it," their issues of self-esteem are not well understood. "Think of how much a Black person has to sell of himself to try to get race not to matter. . . . You have to ignore the natural loyalties. You have to ignore your past. In a sense, you have to just about deny yourself."[7]

In low-income neighborhoods, the storefront church may be the primary mental health resource, an agency of moral guidance and social control. For example, storefront churches have been integral to inner-city life for decades. There, inner-city residents join with others to sing soul-stirring melodies with foot-stomping rhythms. They move to the beat of drums, shouting and singing their longing for dignity and respect in the face of violence, racism, and discrimination.[8]

But this is not true for everyone. Some are spiritual refugees from the church—individuals who no longer feel that their spiritual needs are being met by established religious institutions, or have been made to feel unwelcomed, persecuted, and/or driven from their customary place of worship and feel spiritually home-less. They feel driven away, yet see themselves as spiritual beings who are related to the Supreme being but no longer attend church. For others, religion and the church are irrelevant. The church is dis-dained and distrusted by many young people who see the church as preoccupied with another world, and in this world it seems too poor and powerless against the forces that rule their lives. While many African American youth succeed in school, many more, es-pecially inner-city youth, experience public school failure. Early in life they learn the strategies and values of street survival. They often drop out of school and into trouble with the law. Their involve-ment in the criminal justice system may begin early and progress through detention, county jail, and prison. Many face early preg-nancy, chronic unemployment, and poverty. When employment op-portunities arise, they are not prepared to compete in the job mar-ket or to make their way through legitimate channels of success. There are exceptions, and many of these problems are endemic to American society. Many whites have been alienated and impover-ished, and other nonwhite minorities are greatly disadvantaged by the workings of the American mainstream. Together, the unem-ployed and impoverished from different ethnic backgrounds reflect America's failures to achieve equality—even through such mea-sures as affirmative action programs. Affirmative action is a gov-ernment policy that attempts to redress the racial imbalance in col-leges and the workplace by increasing the number of persons from underrepresented groups. It is a form of positive discrimination that favors those from disadvantaged groups who are ready to take advantage of opportunities when the doors open. Affirmative ac-tion, however, has not helped those who are greatly disadvantaged, such as the working poor or the very poor. Problems of the inner city reveal the cumulative effects of racism and of discriminatory practices in social institutions and public policies—and the cost is reflected in personal lives. Among the personal and structural prob-lems are teenage pregnancies, spousal and child abuse, indiscrimi-nate use of guns, a pervasive sense of despair, low self-esteem and, perhaps, the growth of permanent marginalized groups within our democracy.[9] The effects have been a deepening sense of hopelessness and emptiness, an attachment to surrogate material values, detachment from spiritual values, and a deepening ethical and spiritual crisis. If this is the case for an increasing number of African American family members, then how can the tapping of spiritual resources help in situations like these?

In this light, Auerswald draws attention to cognitive growth, which is a part of the spiritual resources to be developed. Cognitive development refers to the intellectual skills and processes that enable us to know, understand, and cooperate with others in shaping a more just society. Spiritual questions and ideas are part of cognitive development. They are instrumental in helping to address questions in which children and adults have a profound interest. Spiritual questions and ideas help us to locate ourselves in time and space, to figure out who we are, where we come from, where we are going, and what is the purpose or meaning of our lives.[10] Consider the following examples of cognitive and spiritual development through children's experiences. A child once asked, "What happens to the moon when you can't see it? Where does it go?" Another child asked, "Why do people do mean things?" A five-year-old came home from school one day and with a sense of alarm in her voice asked her mother, "Who is God?!" The questions *who, what, why, where,* and *when* are among the basic questions that children raise about their world. When they do so, they are engaged in an exercise of cognitive, moral, and spiritual development. Robert Coles, a child psychiatrist, made the observation, "There is a natural overlap between the moral life and the religious life of children, as is the case with grownups. There is certainly an overlap for many children between their religious life and their spiritual life—even for young people who have never set foot in any religious institution or received any religious instruction whatsoever."[11] Valerie M. DeMarinis, a pastoral psychotherapist, tells the story of Heather.[12] Heather was a young child struggling to make sense out of her images of God. In Sunday church school she drew a picture of God as male and female. Her picture was crossed out and rejected when presented to her teacher because it did not fit the teacher's image of God. DeMarinis reports how this confusing rejection of Heather's early expressions of her faith by an adult and an authority figure was later corrected when she was encouraged by a therapist to look again at her drawing and find value in it. This experience of imaging God was a part of Heather's spiritual and cognitive development. On one occasion, I made a transatlantic flight and arrived at my destination in the morning. Friends met me at the airport, and with them was their seven-year-old grandson. That evening, he asked his grandmother, Why did that man who came for dinner not come in the evening? Why did he have to come in the morning? This child was engaged in an exercise of cognitive development by trying to put order in his experience and give it meaning.

All of the children above were struggling with abstract ideas, purpose, and meaning. Cognitive development has to do with making sense of events, principles, rules, abstract concepts, values, and purpose. These skills are building blocks for problem solving, making connections, anticipating consequences, and cooperation. When children stop their play to argue over the rules of the game, they are involved in an exercise of cognitive, moral, and spiritual development. When they are in conflict and try to distinguish right from wrong, good from bad, they are involved in an exercise of cognitive development and moral reasoning. In this way, they come to see themselves as others see them. They come to develop moral schemes for living that include or exclude others. Ideally, they learn the skills of cooperation and develop a capacity for critical thinking, introspection, and self-correction—in relations with others.

Auerswald emphasized cognitive growth and self- differentiation in infant-child-adolescent-adult development in a time of social reform (the 1960s), when economic and cultural development was stressed. Underemphasized was the balance of influences between the economic and cultural environment on one hand and cognitive development on the other. This balance of influences, which Auerswald referred to as the "interface between" the external and internal environment, is the key to growth and effective social participation. This interface is becoming increasingly complex in secular urban environments.

At the center of our concern is the family, which is challenged to help the infant grow from infancy to childhood to adolescence to adulthood. This challenge is made difficult when the neighborhood or immediate environment that surrounds the family is dangerous. And it is especially dangerous for young black men and women between the ages of fifteen and thirty-four. For them, the leading cause of death is homicide. The homes in which some infants and toddlers are raised are exposed to the same dangers that exist in the neighborhood. A stray bullet entering the room and killing or severely injuring an infant lying it its crib may be only one of many ways a child is vulnerable. In such a situation, neighborhood violence also becomes a family tragedy.

Still, one of the most important needs is to nurture bonds of attachment and to instill a sense of belonging, self-worth, and reciprocity, or mutual give and take, in the growing person. The growing person, in her or his turn, will develop the skills, knowledge, and language that contribute to self-identity and contribute to the life of the family and wider society. The key to learning and the integration of experience is the capacity to participate in the life of the group and to experience oneself as a valued member. The family plays the crucial role in the infant-child-adolescent-adult development in that it is the original environment where one comes to know oneself. Cultural patterns and gender roles are transmitted through family relationships and internalized. Over time, communication and behavior patterns or messages are elaborated and repeated in the interaction between the person, the neighborhood, and wider society. They become integrating themes of selfhood. "The degree to which a child will develop a sufficiently differentiated view of reality to assure his effective adaptation to the large variety of differing life situations with which he will be presented in our complex and changing society will depend on the quantity, and quality, clarity, and differentiation, according to life operations, of the 'integrating themes' around which he organizes himself."[13] The important point is that the family plays the crucial role in the process of balancing the forces between the person and the system. The family is where the individual first comes to self-knowledge, learns to label the environment, names abstract concepts such as rules and values, organizes experience, and cooperates with others to help create meaning in life.[14]

Where families are not able to play this crucial role of helping to balance social influences and personal experience, then the child will be lacking in cognitive growth, will be diminished in skills for making it in society, and will be vulnerable to a repeated sense of failure and despair. Because families in secular society find it increasingly difficult to perform the crucial role of balancing external and internal influences, it is important to focus on the interface between the family and the workings of the wider society. African American culture, in its many manifestations, has been the important interface between family members and the wider society. It has been a source for positive self-images—such as "Black is beautiful," and "You are somebody." It has carried the collective memory, the rich oral and written stories of struggle, tragedy, and survival, proverbs, traditions of care, role models, and critical reflection. It is a source for conjuring hope and strategies for living. By "conjuring" I mean improvising or inventing something through magical means, or evoking an image or a memory, or making contact with the spirit world through performing certain acts for the purpose of curing or harming. African American culture in its many manifestations is a resource that must not be ignored by the knowledgeable help giver who works with African American families. In this light, how can the therapist learn to draw out, help to mobilize, positively value, and contribute to the renewal of spiritual traditions and resources that empower family members to live through times like these?

Harbingers of Hope

Most family therapists operate from a sense of justice. Many have a systemic orientation to family therapy, yet they may not be trained in theological and spiritual disciplines. Still, they may ask the discerning question, How can the above-mentioned social conditions be turned around when such conditions are not currently a priority of social and economic policies or health care reforms? That question has theological import. It is like asking, Where or to whom does one turn and find hope when the tide of despair is rising? Family therapists, like pastors, can be harbingers of hope when they collaborate with African American families around spiritual values. They bring hope when they enable critical reflection and spiritual discernment, increase a sense of moral agency, and draw upon the family's cultural heritage and spiritual resources. To engage help seekers in this way offers them an opportunity to examine how their often unexamined, yet deeply held, beliefs work with their behavior. It provides an opportunity to use their imagination, evolve their beliefs, and integrate belief and behavior.

The human-Divine relationship is our great resource, and hope lies in relationships that enable us to make connections, nurture a sense of self-worth, stimulate the imagination, and support the dogged struggle to humanize social and economic policies and institutions. Rosa Parks provides an example of humanizing an institutionalized practice when she tells of a city ordinance that was passed in Dearborn, Michigan, in 1985. It was instituted to restrict the use of a public park to white residents. The effect of this ordinance was to keep nonwhites out. Why would they do this on the one hand and "welcome our dollars in their stores," on the other hand? Drawing inspiration from the freedom struggles of the 1950s and 1960s, Parks, along with others, made connections between unjust practices and strategies for change. As a result they were able to effect change and help bring greater justice. They did this by meeting in churches, naming the issues, and planning. They had a shared sense that their cause was just. They organized to carry out their strategies. They drew strength through shared memories of former struggles, inspirational singing, prayers, and Scripture readings. In this way they were able to keep up the struggle until the desired change was effected. "As long as people use tactics to oppress or restrict other people from being free, there is work to be done. Although we have made many gains, racism is still alive."[15] Hope lies in the collective struggle to remove the stumbling blocks of racism. It derives from opportunities to grow and participate in the ongoing transformation of society. African American families can be empowered to humanize the institutions and processes in which they participate when they see hope.

The transformation of the North American mainstream requires the working together of the spiritual and material resources in concert with the freedom struggles of all the people. Family therapists can learn to attend to the cultural heritage, spiritual beliefs, and metaphors that underlie family struggles.

Key Resources for Navigation

There are other books on the topics of family therapy, psychotherapy, spirituality, and African American pastoral care. Indebted to these but with an altered agenda, I will highlight three interpretive tools that are important for understanding families in their relationship to culture, spiritual resources, and themselves. The three tools are dimension of depth, reflexivity, and sense of agency. By the dimension of depth, I mean the spiritual legacy of African American families with its origins in the deep river of African American history, culture, and freedom struggles. The meaning and usefulness of a family's spiritual legacy is deepened as they remember it, come to know it better, internalize its values, and contribute to its growth.

Self-reflexivity is the individual's developing capacity for solitude, conjuring, critical thinking, seeing oneself through the eyes of another, introspection, and self-correction. Reflexivity becomes social when family members get a glimpse of themselves as a group interacting with other families or standards. Social reflexivity is the family's way of mirroring itself through self-questioning, humor, stories that are shared, assessment or reassessment of their institutions, values, and goals.

Sense of agency is the ongoing struggle to bring about beneficial change that makes a difference. To have a sense of agency is to act with intent or purpose and with the belief that one can produce an effect or influence an outcome. Through participation and repeated acts of mutual care a person may become able to counter despair, bring change, and help transform social conditions. The phrase "a sense of" implies self-consciousness, the belief that one's efforts can be self-directed.[16]

The three interpretive tools—dimension of depth, reflexivity, and sense of agency—are used in two ways. First, as descriptions of the family's capacities and key resources. Second, to describe the work of the therapist. I use these three tools in both the first and second ways, which I shall explain.

First, it is assumed that African American families, and all families, have a shared cultural heritage as well as a familial legacy. I shall refer to this as the deep river of African American spirituality. It has its origins in the ancient past and winds its way through the present toward a future that it shares with all of humankind. African Americans are the descendants of an ancient African civilization rich in cultural diversity, tribal and kinship traditions, religion and the arts, law, education, and mythology. African Americans have cultural traditions with roots in the Caribbean and in East and West Africa, as well as in the United States. They have inherited the lessons of struggle, of resistance, of living and dying. These lessons, which are a part of the collective memory, help constitute spiritual resources that come from the past and are given new meaning in the present. The confluence of spiritual resources is the deep river that sustains hope and provides resources for removing the stumbling blocks of racism and other forms of oppression. Navigating this deep river is what gives a family depth of meaning and hope. Family members construct their own sense of agency as individuals and as a family unit as they navigate this deep river. As individuals, family members have a sense of their own contribution to the family unit and can enable certain things to happen, such as protecting, caring for, and comforting one another. As a family unit, they can contribute to a collective ethos that makes the family feel like a safe place (or an unsafe place). Reflexivity is the individual or family capacity to review what has happened and find the courage to continue or to change. Reflexivity is also the individual or family capacity to preview, i.e., anticipate certain consequences. In short, dimension of depth or depth of meaning, reflexivity, and sense of agency are used to describe resources and capacities within the family and within black culture. These resources are essential to personal and social transformation.

Second, depth of meaning, reflexivity, and sense of agency are part of the work of the therapist. The therapeutic goal may be to tap the spiritual resources of African American families. In this way, the therapist may enable families or family members to deepen meaning in life as they (family members) increase affection for one another, develop their sense of respect, fair play, and acceptance and grow together through the good times and the bad.

This book builds on the assumption that the family, and the church as the representative religious institution, hold the key to the survival and well-being of black people in American society. It is a book for family therapists, pastors, seminarians, and other caregivers who work or expect to work with African American families in a multicultural society. It is intended to help workers use the religious beliefs, spiritual experiences, artistic expressions, and metaphors of African American culture and families as a resource vital to mental well-being, successful therapy, and spiritual growth. It is a resource for personal and social transformation.

A woman told of her navigating experience: "I got sick of myself and the things that were happening in my life. There was nothing good there." So she returned to the storefront church where her mother and stepfather worship. She said, "I like living right. It's a lot of security being in church. It's an experience and understanding of life and its problems that you can't explain."[17] For some, her faith may appear to be naive or insufficiently examined. But it is *her* faith. It moved her from being a person "sick of myself" and leading an insecure life to one with a sense of security and a new connection with family members. If her faith can continue to do that, then she has reason to hope. If her life can be renewed, then she can be an agent for positive change in the lives of others.

The questions I pursue are: How can African American individuals and families find strength within themselves and deepen life's meaning as they continue to evolve in a society that enslaved them? How can therapists learn from work with African American families, as they seek to promote reflexivity and a sense of agency, aid the development of meaning, and help to deepen a sense of purpose in life? This book, then, has three objectives: (1) to heighten awareness of the continuous interplay between personal and family troubles, the operation of historical forces and workings of the larger social system, and spiritual resources; (2) to demonstrate how the African American family and its spiritual resources are a strength to be tapped by the informed counselor; (3) to demonstrate that the use of metaphor is central to working with African

American families—especially the river metaphor, which will be introduced to complement the well-known systems metaphor.

The river metaphor will be utilized to tap the spiritual resources of African American families. I use the river metaphor in several ways. First, I use it as a metaphor for the workings of American society as a whole. Therefore, I refer to American society as the mainstream, the great water system of which we are part. Second, I use the river as a metaphor for a description of family life process, and for the ongoing life of individual family members. Therefore, I refer to the droplets of experience that help to constitute the stream of experiences that bind African American families together or tear them apart. Hence, life experience is described as an experiential stream, and as a branch of the mainstream of American society. Third, I refer to all families as rivers that have their differing points of origin within the wider, multicultural society in general and black culture in particular. All have different journeys, but all of them flow to the sea.

The river can provide the resources to transform the stumbling blocks of racism and poverty, and enable us to remain strong and hopeful. Common to each of these different uses of the river metaphor is the idea of water as a basic element of life and renewal, and the river as an ecosystem that gives, nurtures, carries, and takes life. The river transforms itself even as it is being transformed on its journey. The sea is the river's destination and source. It contains the basic elements to renew us in the ongoing struggle to humanize and help transform society. The river flows through us, the sea surrounds us.[18]

~

1

> *For our struggle is not against enemies of blood and*
> *flesh, but against the rulers, against the authorities,*
> *against cosmic powers of this present darkness,*
> *against spiritual forces of evil in the heavenly place.*
>
> Ephesians 6:12s

This chapter argues the idea of African American families as changing, resilient, and adaptive rather than static in response to the American mainstream. Therefore, their strengths, weaknesses, and function must be assessed with reference to the economic system and historical forces operating in the American mainstream.

Imagine a family of 12, with ages ranging from 1 to 38 years. The family head is a single adult female. The family represents three generations, and they live together in a three-room apartment. They try to survive on welfare income. Family members live in a neighborhood where unemployment is high. The neighborhood itself is comprised of low-income apartments, with families living at or below the poverty line, absent landlords, and vacant buildings. The streets and homes are made unsafe by burglary, drug trafficking, and rape and other forms of violent crime. Police protection is negligent. The school dropout rate is high. Barber shops, beauty salons, cleaners, and grocery stores are among the few businesses that remain in the neighborhood. Public transportation is not easily accessible. The family has little hope that things will change for the better. Perhaps their hope is that things will not get worse, or maybe someone might get lucky and hit the lottery, and then things will change for the better. Many families are in that situation today. How representative are they? Do they constitute a permanent underclass, a self-perpetuating culture of poverty? Are such families in a state of disintegration . . . or is there something else to be discerned here?

In his book *Climbing Jacob's Ladder,* the sociologist Andrew Billingsley makes the point that black life and black families in America must be understood in the light of broad historical, cultural, social, economic, and political forces that are shaping American society.[1] On the one hand, broad influences are responsible for creating a variety of family forms, such as nuclear, extended, and augmented families. On the other hand, family members make their own unique adaptive responses to the conflicting demands of the larger society. Billingsley places emphasis on black working-class families, but at the same time his analysis is inclusive of "two-parent families, single-parent families, and no-parent families. It includes upper-income as well as middle- and low-income families. It embraces highly achieving families as well as marginal and troubled families."[2] Families are strong and weak by turns, but they are essentially resilient and change throughout their life cycle. Billingsley does not attribute the origins of family structure or organization to family pathology or to a self-perpetuating culture of poverty—independent of society. Rather, family structures evolve as adaptations to the workings of society.

My family of origin may be described as black working class. If we were evaluated by the standards of white society, then we looked weak in terms of educational standing, job status, and material wealth. Both parents worked, my father as a manual laborer and my mother as a domestic. My mother had a high-school education, and my father had achieved the eighth grade. They owned their own home and raised five children. After my parents settled in Seattle in the 1930s, our household frequently increased and decreased in size and changed in structure over time as family members migrated from the Deep South to the Pacific Northwest. Cousins, uncles, aunts, and grandparents moved in and lived with us until they were in a position to move out and into their own home or apartment. Children were born, relatives became ill, some died. Others experienced loss of jobs as our nuclear family swelled to be an augmented family, and then contracted to a nuclear family again. As we children came of age and left home, our family size shrunk. Our parents retired, one died, a few of the children move back home and left again for personal and economic reasons. Grandchildren moved in and then moved out on their own. The sense of family was adaptive and changed dramatically over time.

The church community my parents joined was made up of families that had migrated from the South. They shared a common belief in the parenthood of God and the kinship of all people, although they did not say it like that. It was common to hear them refer to each other as brother and sister, and to the pastor as brother or sister pastor. The church family became our extended family over time. The members provided spiritual, emotional, intellectual, and sometimes financial resources that augmented our own. As a result, the children, as well as the adults, were exposed to a range of role models. We observed men and women expressing strong emotion and handling conflict in different ways.

Family size is a function of historical and economic shifts on the one hand, and adaptive responses on the other. My family was part of a larger group of African Americans who migrated from the South to urban centers in the North during the 1930s and 1940s in search of jobs, affordable housing, and opportunity. "The structure of African American family life is purposive, that is, it is not accidental, haphazard, or mysterious."[3] The family's adaptive responses can modify or extend existing family structures, or generate new ones. Billingsley's main point is that the larger society impacts family viability in positive and negative ways; and family structure and patterns are not static. They change over time and in response to changes in the wider society. The basic purpose of the family is to meet the developing physical, emotional, cognitive, and spiritual needs of its members as best it can, and to respond to change. The family's adaptive capacities, supported by resources within African American communities, is to be emphasized. "The resourceful black grandmother, the vital black church, the effective

3

black school, the successful black business enterprise, the authentic black scholar, the hardworking, long-suffering black masses, the upwardly mobile sectors: all hold important keys to the regeneration of our families, our communities, and our society."[4] It is necessary to see the interplay of all of these influences—they are mediating influences that stand between the child or individual on the one hand, and the impact of society on the other.

Some observers of the African American family have viewed it as resulting from a culture of poverty or pathological processes, in a state of disintegration or vanishing, rather than adaptive and changing in response to the working of the American mainstream. The message for pastoral caregivers and therapists is to appreciate the adaptive responses that black families make to the pressures on them and to recognize that African American families are dynamic and are characterized by a wide variety of structures.

Billingsley further argued that black families are best understood when compared with all African American families as a whole. This may include mixed-race families. When white families are used as the norm for interpreting the life of black people and their families, then misunderstandings arise and a distorted picture of black families often results. Therefore, black families are best understood in relationship to themselves, and as resilient institutions responding to broad historical and social forces that are shaping the American mainstream. In this light, the responses that families make are adaptations to the interpersonal and wider influences that are shaping the whole of American life.

Billingsley's work is valuable for a number of reasons. First, he challenges views of the black family that use, uncritically, a white standard as the norm for everyone. Second, his perspective is supported by a careful interpretation of statistical data derived from the U.S. Bureau of the Census, and further corroborated with the findings of other social scientists who are students of African American families.

Billingsley's contribution ought to inform the therapist's work with African American families. It underscores the importance of understanding the larger picture of how African American families and the American mainstream interrelate.

Using Billingsley's contribution as a guide, we return to our imaginary family to envision how a therapist or pastoral counselor might work. In so doing we note several levels to this work. First is the level of questions that would help the therapist develop awareness of the wider picture that surrounds the family. Second is the level of the interface between the family and the surrounding society. Third is the level of work with the family.

At the first level, the emphasis is on developing awareness of the ecological system, or wider environment, that surrounds and interacts with the family. Prior to contact with the family it would be important to have some firsthand impressions of the neighborhood and its evolution. The following questions would be useful to help orient the therapist: What families appear to be functioning well and how are they going about that? What recent changes has the neighborhood undergone? What is the aesthetics or visual impact of this neighborhood today? How safe are the streets by day and by night? What role does (or should) law enforcement play? How accessible are jobs, recreation, transportation, and grocery stores and other small businesses that neighborhood residents depend on for their daily needs? Where do people tend to gather? Where are the hospitals or clinics, churches, schools, and taverns located? Who are the community leaders? How do community decisions get made and who participates in that process? How do residents influence city and government agencies? What kind of housing is available? How do people typically spend their time? What are the many ways cash flows in and out of the community? How are federal funds and programs involved? What social policies benefit or work against community development? Who represents this district in the U.S. House or Senate? These are only some of the questions that might help orient the therapist to the neighborhood. More questions can be identified as the therapist's knowledge of the neighborhood evolves.

At the next level of that interface, the emphasis is on the interaction *between* the family and the wider environment. It would be important to know how our imaginary family fits in and relates to the rest of the neighborhood. How safe are they? When someone attempts to break in and do harm, how do they protect themselves from external violence? What is their relationship to kin? Where do they (kin) live? Many institutions exist in the surrounding society.

What institutions are most involved in the life of this family? In what organized activities do they participate outside the family? What avenues need to be opened and connections established in order for family members to have wider access and a chance at making it?

At the family level, the emphasis is on how the family understands itself and interacts with the environment. This imaginary family might come to the attention of the therapist by way of referral—from school, the courts, a minister, social worker, concerned neighbor—or through direct contact with a family member. If it is decided that the therapist's first meeting should be with the family in their home, then it would be important to know what concern necessitates the therapist's presence, who is raising the concern, and what family members are most (or least) affected by it. Who should attend that first meeting—i.e., what colleague should accompany the therapist? What would be the role of the companion colleague?

Before meeting each member of our hypothetical family, it would be important for the therapist to establish rapport with the family head, gain her permission, and enlist her cooperation in work with her family. It would be important to find out what is going on within the family here and now. What concerns or needs are being expressed now? How engaged or disengaged is the parental figure? What is needed to empower her? What specific direction or support can the therapist give now? It would be important to know how the family manages 12 people, ages 1 to 38 years, in the space of three rooms. For some, this would be an impossible feat. How does the family manage it? How do they interact with one another? What kinds of roles are available to them? How do they talk to one another, argue, handle differences, express strong emotion, and manage stress or trauma? What health-care, cognitive, emotional, and self-esteem needs do family members present? What has already been done to address them? What values do they espouse, what are their shared beliefs, and how is spirituality expressed? It would be important to know how family members care for one another and make use of community resources, where their strengths are and how they use them. What, if anything, are family members interested in changing and what are the resources for effecting change? What is the family hierarchy and what subsystems exist? How flexible or rigid are the subsystems, and the boundaries between them? These are a few concerns that could be raised initially at the level of the family.

The above is only an imaginary sketch devised to demonstrate how Billingsley's concern would push us beyond the traditional approaches and techniques of psychotherapy, treatment, and counseling. His contribution results in awareness of how social and historical conditions influence family structure and support or hinder the therapist's intervention. Traditional approaches that have emphasized talk therapy and insight as the basis for change have often failed the kind of family represented in our imaginary scenario.

The important point is that the family exists within an ecological system, and change cannot be effected by working with the family alone as if they were separate from their environment. It is important to develop a frame of reference for our work. A disadvantaged population is a heterogeneous group with diverse needs. What might work with one disadvantaged family may not work with another. Therefore, it is dangerous to generalize from one family to the next. Families manifest different needs, styles, and cognitive approaches to problem solving. The identified levels and questions mentioned above will enable a therapist to see similarities and differences between families. It is important, then for the therapist to find a way to build information, a frame of reference that can account for similarities and diversity, challenge social myths, and remain open to different information and approaches.[5]

It is rare when social and historical analysis is included in the therapist's training or preparation for work with the family life of African Americans. Therapists usually begin with the presenting problem and trace it to factors in the person's psychological makeup, or family of origin, or family of creation. Family therapists may focus on family structure, processes, or the transmission of transgenerational influences, but not necessarily on developing multilevel or systemic awareness.

How does the present book differ from Billingsley's *Climbing Jacob's Ladder*? As a sociologist, Billingsley is concerned with the formal and informal power arrangements within society over time. He is concerned with the way society creates the conditions that favor or constrain social groups according to certain perceived characteristics such as race or ethnicity, class, gender, sexual orientation, and age. My concern as a pastoral caregiver and social psychologist is both similar and different. Similar, inasmuch as I too am concerned with the cumulative effects of social power arrangements over time. Different, inasmuch as I focus on the *interaction between* the workings of the larger society and the people who struggle from day to day to make their lives meaningful.

I focus on processes of internalization that result in negative or positive images of the self and others. I worked primarily with inner-city youth and their families when I served as minister-to-the-community and pastoral counselor while on staff at the First Baptist Church of Worcester, Massachusetts. My goal with the youth was to work with self-image and self-esteem issues, broaden their horizons, and enable them to succeed in school. I did this by building a personal relationship with young men and women by visiting with them in their homes and at play in recreational facilities, by school visits, and by meeting with them in my home. I involved them in the planning of weekend retreats. In a safe environment away from the city, they could engage in small-group discussions about the issues that concerned them as teenagers. Black and white professionals such as medical doctors, psychologists, educators, law enforcement officials, social workers, and ministers, male and female, were invited to make presentations at the retreat site and engage the youth in informal conversation. The professionals were mainly there as accessible role models. Many of them had grown up in the community. I adopted this way of working because many of the young women and men welcomed it. Exposure to positive role models was an important part of their development. Many of the youth I came to know had been in trouble with the law and were in trouble at school. Some of them believed that society was against them and they would not succeed. At the retreat site, they could meet others who felt similarly when they were young but were now professionals who contributed to the community. Working with these representatives of society in an informal retreat setting of give-and-take over time helped young men and women to envision new possibilities for their lives. Some years later, I still have contact with one of those teenagers, who is now a woman in her early forties. She is a university graduate and a community worker in a position to influence other young people. I continue to build on my learning from the work I did with those young people. I also make hospital, jail, home, school, and church visits with some of the young people and their families who are in therapy with me today.

My concept of therapy is broad and context-dependent. It is informed by a black church spiritual tradition that views personal and social transformation as interrelated in the reality of God. The well-being of the individual is interwoven with the well-being of the whole community. Therefore, therapy includes different levels of activity. It is not limited to talk therapy, psychological intervention, or personal change, although it includes these. The term "therapeutic" refers to the art of healing and methods of curing a wound or relieving suffering. But what are the levels of suffering? The suffering may be spiritual, emotional-psychological, physical, or historical—that is, long-term. It may be social-economic or a combination of these. Curative methods may range from one-to-one talk therapy to large-scale social-political action, such as the mid-twentieth-century civil rights movement in the United States. This was a movement aimed at transforming long-term and entrenched sources of suffering. Methods such as boycotts, strikes, and other forms of nonviolent action can help to end certain forms of suffering, bring new awareness, psychic release, change and healing in relationships, and social cohesion. At the same time there may be a need to work through the implications of such change at the personal level, or in relation to family members. Curative methods differ from time to time and from culture to culture. Groups and individuals respond differently to curative measures. Basic to my concept of therapy is the belief that curative methods are strategies that we employ in order to effect change or healing. Healing, itself, is something that comes from beyond us and is an experience of the human-divine relationship. The Divine Spirit is the bearer of healing. People can attempt to impede or help to mobilize the Spirit's healing activity, but they cannot control it. Some people have been culturally designated and trained to mobilize curative resources, such as the shaman, the medical doctor, the priest, or the psychotherapist. Curative and corrective measures also come through other kinds of relationships, such as friendship or the teacher-student relationship. Therapeutic communities (such as the church, synagogue, mosque, or rehabilitation center) exist and provide resources necessary to mobilize therapeutic change. Sometimes, religious revivals or large-scale social-change movements help to bring about therapeutic effects when collective suffering is ended and people are able to live in a different or more just relationship to one another. Harriet Tubman, the emancipator and famous "conductor" of the Underground Railroad, was a therapeutic agent who challenged the evils of white supremacy, helping others to escape the brutal conditions of slavery and make it to freedom. Therapeutic change presupposes the question of the direction of the change. Change for what? Not all change is for the better, and not all change counters oppressive practices, or serves the aims of wider justice, or fosters the emergence of democratic communities. Therefore, therapeutic change, as I envision it, must also be concerned with purpose, moral character, the selves that we are becoming through our decisions and activity, and the kind of society we create together. Family therapy is just one level of therapeutic activity, and it is linked to and affected by changes at other levels.[6]

I refer to my way of working as *systemic,* that is, I make connections *between* events (e.g., trouble at school) and the corresponding shifts that take place *within* people (i.e., self-esteem) and their family relations. Therefore, it is not necessary to choose between the work of the sociologist and that of the social psychologist. Both the sociologist and social psychologist are concerned with social location, i.e., how one's position and activities in society shape what one sees or does not see, and what one reports or fails to report. Since the work of the sociologist and social psychologist overlaps, it is not wise to draw too rigid a boundary between their interests. Both can inform the pastoral counselor and family therapist about the American mainstream. This is discussed in the next chapter.

~

2

NAVIGATING SPIRITUAL IMPOVERISHMENT

IN THE AMERICAN MAINSTREAM

> *A pervasive spiritual impoverishment grows. The
> collapse of meaning in life—the eclipse of hope and
> absence of love of self and others, the breakdown of
> family and neighborhood bonds—leads to the social
> deracination and cultural denudement of urban
> dwellers, especially children. We have created rootless,
> dangling people with little links to the supportive
> net-works—family, friends, school—that sustain
> some sense of purpose in life.*
>
> *. . . it is no surprise that the notion that we are
> all part of one garment of destiny is discredited.*
>
> *What is to be done? How do we capture a new
> spirit and vision to meet the challenges of the post-
> industrial city, post-modern culture, and post-party
> politics?*
>
> Cornel West, *Race Matters*

This chapter extends the argument of chapter 1 and identifies ideological forces that shape understandings of African Americans and
family life. This chapter also raises questions about the direction of
the American mainstream.

American society is the large river system. The waters of the large river system are the people, traditions, cultures, beliefs and practices, and many institutions that constitute the society.[1] The African American family is a stream within the great river system. Hence the questions: Where have we been? Where are we going? Where are we now? In short, what is our location within the large river system of American society? African Americans once shared a common sense of purpose and role in America. A shared sense of purpose and role were taught or caught in the family as family members shared their experiences with one another and as the children sat at the feet of the elders and listened intently to the stories being narrated. The young people learned lessons about resistance, escape from slavery to freedom, and the struggle to humanize society. For example, my parents were part of a generation of African Americans whose primary concern was to be free from white control, to vote, and to give their children educational opportunities that were denied them. They left Mississippi and settled in the Pacific Northwest, hoping that their children would have a better chance in this society. They joined a black church, where their hopes for the future found support and stories of their experience could be shared. Their main message was "prepare yourself to make a contribution to society and help lift someone else." My mother was the one who instilled the idea that self-help was linked with the help of others. Whenever we went to the store we were expected to see if anyone else needed something as well. She taught us, by example and instruction, to see the connection between our needs and the needs of others. In this way, a shared sense of purpose was taught and caught. This practice of seeing the link between one's own needs and the needs of others is part of systemic thinking and it is critical to the future of African Americans.

Systemic thinking is a way to view individuals and their behavior as always embedded in a specific context and a wider social system. It views social systems as organized over time, the reciprocity between the members, and the meanings they coconstruct by virtue of their context and relationship to time, place and role. It is part of envisioning the future and the transformation of a democratic society.

Mutual care is a practice that counters selfishness, greed, and spiritual impoverishment, which appears to be growing. A sense of purpose or role was further articulated in various ways by our leaders, by the spirituals and gospels, by poetry, and by sports and literary figures. They gave us direction and hope. In short, role models were to be found inside and outside the family. The collective struggle against race discrimination and other forms of violence gave hope.

It is important to note that leaders such as Harriet Tubman, Sojourner Truth, W. E. B. DuBois, Rosa Parks, Viola Luizzo, Martin Luther King Jr., Malcolm X, Fannie Lou Hamer, and many, many others struggled to humanize and transform the American mainstream. They struggled for the good of all the people, and not just for themselves. Theirs was a struggle for inclusion and wider justice. In the early part of this century W. E. B. DuBois argued that the color line was the problem of the twentieth century. Martin Luther King Jr. thought that the major obstacles were injustice and discrimination. He thought the solution resided in a new kind of a community, an open, integrated society where people of different backgrounds would no longer be judged by the color of their skin, but by the content of their character. In his memorable "I Have a Dream" speech given in Washington, D.C., in 1963, King conjured an ideal version of the American mainstream. King believed that nonviolent struggle was the way to humanize social institutions and help transform society. At the same time, he was consistently deepening his critique of the economic arrangements of United States society. He was increasingly calling for economic democracy, especially in the post-1963 years.[2]

Malcolm X struggled for the good of others. He saw that the major issue standing in the way of humanization for black people was a lack of power, self-definition, and collective self-determination. He did not believe that those who were on top would relinquish power nonviolently. He felt that black people needed to consider all options, which included violence, if necessary. Hence, self-determination would be achieved "by any means necessary." James Cone argued that Martin and Malcolm struggled unselfishly as they pursued different strategies. They struggled for the same goal of freedom and a transformed society.

> Martin's and Malcolm's movement toward each other is a clue
> that neither can be fully understood nor appreciated without se-
> rious attention to the other. They complemented and corrected
> each other, each spoke a truth about America that cannot be fully
> comprehended without the insights of the other. Indeed, if
> Americans of all races intend to create a just and peaceful future,
> then they must listen to both Martin and Malcolm.[3]

Martin and Malcolm represented different ideological strains within
U.S. society. They believed in the absolute necessity of struggle for
change. Both were strenuously engaged in the transformation of the
North American mainstream and black America's role in it.

In his helpful book *Black Religious Leaders: Conflict in Unity,*
the social ethicist Peter J. Paris compared the contribution of several
civil rights leaders on the question of race.[4] Rather than view the
mid-century civil rights leaders as merely competitive, divisive, and
locked into a malign clench, and therefore unable to move the civil
rights struggle forward, Paris viewed each as having an insight, an
angle on a very complex problem facing American society as a
whole. Each offered a partial solution. Taken together, their perspectives contribute to a comprehensive understanding of the problems of racism in United States society. Each was able to draw different parts of the community into the common struggle for justice.
There were multiple roles for African Americans and many ways to
integrate a sense of shared crisis and to experience catharsis. There
could be a complex, yet shared sense of purpose and movement. For
many, therapeutic value and hope came from participation in the
civil rights and social change movement of the 1950s and 1960s.

Black Americans appeared to be united around a common
enemy in the struggle against white racism. Most of us were from
lower, working-class backgrounds, and some of us thought we
were black middle class. A few of us were. But all of us shared experiences of discrimination and race hatred in this society. During
the 1960s, while en route to seminary and driving across the United
States from Seattle, Washington, to Rochester, New York, I passed
a motorist in Minnesota going in the opposite direction. When I
came into view, he held up his middle or index finger. I would have
had to be blind to miss his gesture. It was his sign of hatred, not for

me personally (he did not know me), but toward blacks. It seemed as if every black person had a story to tell about a common experience of race oppression. That is where we have been . . . and still are. Hatred and violence against black people and their institutions is still common.

Integration into the mainstream was the goal held up by many of our parents and by the civil rights struggle of the 1950s and 1960s. But should integration into the white mainstream be the goal for black America? By contrast, separation from the mainstream was the option upheld by Malcolm and his followers. These two agendas of integration and separation continue as unresolved issues in the consciousness of black America. They point in several different directions. Should black families lose hope (as some have), give in to despair, drop out and relinquish the struggle to participate in the American mainstream? Should black families be preparing their young for integration and full participation in the mainstream? Should black families be preparing their young for discernment and self-determination, mutual care, self-reliance, and the strengthening of black institutions? Is there yet another way, one that combines the best of the integrationist-separatist strategies, or are they diametrically opposed? What about the transformation of the mainstream?

In a 1970 publication, the black historian Vincent Harding contrasts "*Negro* History" and "*Black* History."[5] Negro history is defined as an optimistic interpretation of African American presence in United States society that acknowledges their contributions and struggles to enter the mainstream. In this perspective African Americans are essentially the same as white Americans and other groups who have come to American shores. All have been discriminated against in one way or another, and all must strive to improve their situation. This view of Negro history was recently expressed on a radio talk show. The host interviewed a person who identified himself as "black." The radio host asked, "should there be a separate black party to represent the interest of black people?" The black respondent said, "No. White people can represent black people just as well as a black person can represent a white person." Negro history is characterized by optimism, and by the belief that

African Americans can work out their agenda for full acceptance within the basic values and mainstream of white American society. Accordingly, all that is necessary for full acceptance and justice is stated in the Bill of Rights and the Constitution of the United States. The hope of Negro history is that America will someday rise up and live out its creed. This view does not seriously challenge the direction of the mainstream of American society nor does it seek to fundamentally alter its arrangement of power.

The optimism of Negro history eventually gives way to a negative and unreconciled tension. At the heart of Negro history is an internalized sense of black inferiority, belief in white superiority, and the idea that black people with their culture and history have contributed nothing to advance humankind. The tension within Negro history is between the optimistic view that blacks will gradually achieve full acceptance, on the one hand, and the belief in black inferiority and white superiority, on the other hand. The bottom line is that "Negroes" are defined as a people whose primary role is to serve white, Eurocentric interests.

In 1933, Carter Godwin Woodson, an African American educator and historian, summarized Negro history in an exchange between himself and a professor at a Negro college. The professor informed Woodson that courses in Negro history, literature, or race relations are not offered. Rather, "the Negro" is studied in a general way, along with other people. Woodson asked the crucial question of how this is done when "the Negro" is not even mentioned in the textbooks in use at "the Negro college," except in a way that condemns the Negro. The professor mentioned that "the Negro" is referred to here and there throughout the course of study. The college professor, according to Woodson, then made his telling statement: "Negroes have not done much; and what they have accomplished may be briefly covered by referring to the achievements of a few men and women."[6] Such a statement is telling because it results from miseducation or successful brainwashing by the educational system of the white dominant culture. The statement is telling because it mirrors a lack of critical reflection by blacks and whites in positions of influence. Not only do many white people believe in the inherent inferiority of African Americans, but so do many African Americans. They function as agents of white superiority and black inferiority.[7] Ignored is the fact that the dominant white culture's misinformed and negative view of African Americans *is* being taught, minds *are* being shaped, and the status quo goes unchallenged. Ideas about white superiority and black inferiority become institutionalized, that is, a taken-for-granted part of thought and action in everyday living, they form the centerpiece in the dominant system of ideas that mediates the relationship between people in a multicultural society. Such ideas reproduce and help stabilize the structure of relations between groups and appear to be the soundest of ideas for the maintenance of social order.[8] As a result, our so-called free and democratic society, as a whole, is guided by a destructive and dangerous myth that deforms it. When the primary emphasis, for example, is placed on the fact that Abraham Lincoln freed "the Negro" from slavery, it is easy to promote the idea of the white savior. Ignored is the seemingly absurd idea of how the masses of black people in bondage and freedom saved Lincoln. For example, 178,000 African Americans played a critical role in the Civil War when, at last, they were permitted to join the Union forces and help turn the tide of the war. Without them, Lincoln's side may have lost the war.[9] Negro history ignores the significance of African history prior to slavery and the contributions of thousands of black people who continue to help create history. Their experience and ongoing struggle for human freedom is the basis for an alternative vision of society. But this positive view of black experience is beyond the reach of Negro history.

The influence of Negro history is not limited to Carter's observations in the 1930s nor to Harding's in the 1970s. Negro history continues to inform the American mainstream. Negro history has supported the goals of integration and/or black assimilation into white Western societies. It has been seen as the way to move forward. To assimilate means to shed your nonwhite identity, forget the past, and blend into the mainstream of U.S. society. Melt. Assimilation is a goal perceived as both desirable and achievable. It is suggested as a way to transcend racism and the problem of nonwhite exclusion in U.S. society. The appeal of Negro history has an audience that is wider than the United States. Its thought pattern is seen in other countries as well. The attempt to become more like whites has recently claimed the attention of medical doctors in the United Kingdom and parts of Africa. The issue is that millions of black women are using skin-bleaching creams that can cause skin cancer and liver damage. In Gambia, for example, the practice of using skin lightener has been banned by the government. But this has not stopped its use, because there is a high demand for it. *African Express,* a documentary that was aired on British television, reported the widespread use of commercial and homemade bleaching chemicals by many African women.[10] Why do so many African women risk their health to change the color of their skin? it was asked. The answers came back: "Because black is ugly. To change one's skin is to change the ugly look. Then maybe people will like me. I will get ahead and become more successful." For millions, the achievement of lighter skin has become an obsession with devastating effects. It is believed that lighter-skinned people are more desirable and have a better life than people with dark skin. The fact that this is happening in the United Kingdom and parts of Africa points to how widespread the belief is in an assimilationist ideology. It is a by-product of Negro history. The practice is alive and well in the United States, as demonstrated by the use of skin lighteners by multimillionaire pop star Michael Jackson. Many view him as a role model. The message is, change your appearance and fit in with white society. Ironically, many whites try to change the color of their skin through tanning, while some blacks try to change the color of their skin through bleaching. This is not new. The use of creams to lighten the skin was widespread in the United States prior to the black consciousness movement of the 1960s. Those who attempt to assimilate sometimes appear to be more loyal to U.S. society than are many whites who take their citizenship for granted.

A Negro history perspective is not likely to support open criticism of white society, advocate basic reforms, or engage in radical social change movements. This position has roots in slavery. To blend in as far as possible, to be passive and not perceived as a threat, to appear supportive of white superiority, to be guarded, feign ignorance, and appear happy-go-lucky was a way to survive.

Ironically, today, when an African American demonstrates the opposite of this—i.e., shows interest in things intellectual—she or he runs the risk of being thought 'acting uppity' or 'acting white' by both blacks and whites. The point of Negro history is to stay in your place and do not appear to challenge white rule.

A Negro history perspective portrays the economically injured, disadvantaged, or discriminated against as being at fault for not trying hard enough to succeed. The dictum is, if at first you do not succeed, then try, try again. Work harder! Self-reliance, education, and hard work are among the values upheld as the high road to success. Negro history is optimistic because of an unwarranted belief in progress—i.e., the belief that through the achievements of these values (hard work, education, self-reliance) the individual can achieve equality in America. Therefore, there is nothing fundamentally wrong with the way U.S. society works. Whatever contradictions exist will be gradually worked out. Negro history is hard-pressed to answer why those blacks who have made it as individuals—who have graduated from the best professional and graduate schools and who hold the highest degrees and the high-paying jobs—are still behind their counterparts and are still victims of racist discrimination. Perhaps there is truth in the words of a white sociologist who said: "Many whites believe two things—that all people are created equal, and that Blacks are inferior to whites."[11]

From a perspective of Negro history, the proper role of therapy is to help the individual make realistic adjustments within society. Society, itself, is not perceived as the object of change. Societal change is deemed unrealistic and unnecessary. Therefore, emphasis is upon individual change strategies. Pathology, in this view, is located within the individual's mind and plays a major role in behavior. Therefore, therapy aimed at individual change would be the way to help people get ahead or come to terms with contradictions in their personal life. In this view, it is more important to uncover and understand the individual's motives and thinking than to see the interplay between internal mental processes, effects of social power arrangements, and racism. If therapy does not work, it may be because the client did not try hard enough or has not yet acquired the values or skills that would allow her or him to succeed.

Black history departs from the optimism of Negro history and charts a different path. It may be defined as a critical assessment of the events and power arrangements that determine the direction of American society in general and the lives of African Americans in particular. Black history is premised on a deep pessimism concerning American society and holds that African Americans are the best interpreters of their own experience. It is based on a sober and realistic interpretation of the actual experience of the indigenous and black peoples. According to Harding, there is no basis for the belief that justice and full humanity for black people will be achieved in a country controlled and defined by whites. Justice may trickle down for a few, but it will not flow down like a mighty stream. Black people must take control of their own lives and institutions. They must interpret their own history in the light of norms that value and nurture the lives of black people.

This requires reflexivity, a turning back to our past and looking for a new awareness of what our experience has actually been in this country. Reflexivity is a turning back of one's experience upon oneself; or being conscious of ourselves as we see ourselves. Also, seeing ourselves as we are seen by others. It requires a sense of agency that not only reshapes understandings of the past, but inspires activity that builds up a sense of community. Reflexivity aims to build solidarity with other colonized peoples around the world and to support self-determination within the black world. The task of black history, then, is critical reflection on the entire American past. This includes the treatment of the indigenous peoples, Asian Americans, Hispanics, and other ethnic minorities. It includes *exposure* of the deeds and broken promises of white America; *disclosure* of the ways African Americans are currently being deceived and disenfranchised through our own activities—such as the use of skin-bleaching substances, intra-ethnic violence, substance abuse, and other ways that destroy the body, soul, mind, and relationships. Needed is continuous reflection on and a *reinterpretation* of the historical record and our role in it. This process of continuous reflection and self-evaluation can deepen the experience of ourselves as responsible and historically constituted subjects. In Harding's words: "Black History . . . is the facing of the chasm, the hard and unromantic reading of the experiences of Black people in America. It is the groans, the tears, the chains, the songs, the prayers, the institutions, it is a recording of the hopes, even if we no longer participate in them. It is seeing clearly not only what we have done, but what has been done to us. It is the grasping of our history out of the hands of others and taking the responsibility of [people] for the reshaping of our own past."[12]

How would therapy be envisioned from this perspective? The simplest way to state it would be in terms of the ongoing interaction *between* child, family, and society. Attention would be directed to the processes that form the child's developing experiences and expectations in the family; and the many ways society, especially its economic system, influences family structure. Therapy envisioned from a black history perspective would emphasize the interrelationship between historical forces, societal influences, and family structure. It would be sensitive to historical themes that shape African American life and thought, such as the use of spiritual resources in the long history of struggle against racism. It would be sensitive to cultural and relationship themes of freedom and self-determination, a sense of community and self-esteem, creative and artistic response to seemingly hopeless situations. Therapy envisioned from this perspective would utilize family networks and strengths, and seek to understand family difficulties and relations by drawing on family narratives. Narratives may include stories about family members' experiences of victory and defeat in society, as well as stories about relations within the family. Stories of terror and stories of hope would be elicited, as well as stories from the imagination that conjures hope. Pathology would be located in the interactions between family and society, between subsystems within the family, and between family members. The goal of therapy would be to help families to tap their resources, empower them to make desirable change, and contribute to the transformation of social institutions.

The question of African American agency is raised. Is our task to reshape the channel that determines the direction of the river? Reshaping the past was the challenge that Harding saw in the 1970s. The question of agency was the agony facing contemporary black experience. Agony, because within the civil rights movement there were tensions created between the two (Negro and black) views of history. These views appeared to be incompatible. They appeared to point in very different directions and contain different models for reflexivity and self-agency. Hence, tensions *within* society often manifest as tensions *between* family members, and *within* the self. The two views contributed to tensions within African American communities. They contributed to tensions within families, between young and old, and between those who believed in the essential goodness of American institutions and those who did not.

This agony accompanied the struggle for societal transformation that Harding saw. It also created a chasm between white views of history written from a white perspective, which essentially interpreted America as a good and just society, and black views of history, which interpreted mainstream America as an increasingly secular, violent, white-controlled, materialistic society based on utilitarian values and riddled with contradictions. If this was the case, then was the goal of integration into the mainstream a moral and viable option for black Americans? Should there be a different goal, which includes the transformation of society and its values as a whole? If so, then what are the resources for transformation and what are the implications for African American families today? Implied is a role for family therapists and pastoral caregivers who engage with African American families.

Today, African Americans are situated differently in this multiracial and multicultural society. A significant change that the civil rights movement helped to bring about was the vote. African Americans now have the power of the ballot, and we can use it effectively if we have a mind to do so. Another achievement was opening up structures of opportunity. A black man can become the commander of the U.S. armed forces (Colin Powell). An African American can run for president and garner votes from a wider constituency than was possible prior to the civil rights movement (Jesse Jackson ran in 1984, and in 1988 he had support from Midwestern white farmers as well as from urban blacks). Running for president must be distinguished from being elected president. That is a different story! The White House remains elusive. But, even if it were to happen in the United States (i.e., a black person elected president), as it has with Nelson Mandela in South Africa, would that fact alone help to humanize and transform the American mainstream? Many of the visible barriers that kept us from participating fully in this society have been removed. Race discrimination in health care, education, welfare, public housing, and employment is against the law. Avenues of participation that were once closed tight to African Americans have been legally opened.

The critical question remains: namely, what needs to be the direction of this large river system and its values? The workings of American's master institutions benefits the wealthy few and disempowers many other people. The workings of the mainstream often generates despair in society's most vulnerable members. Even with the achievements of the civil rights movement, racism is still on the rise, and subtle forms of discrimination continue to be endemic to every part of U.S. society, including professional mental health associations. The pathological foundation of racism on which this country was built continues to be manifested in clinical training programs, accreditation processes, practice and conferences. Over the years I have attended mental health conferences where, with very few exceptions, there have been only a handful of nonwhites in attendance. Recently, a black colleague reported being one of only two nonwhites present at a mental health conference of about 250 participants. We are still challenged to struggle for the transformation of mainstream institutions and practices, of which mental health is one example. Pastoral caregivers and therapists must identify and continue the struggle against racist practices that contribute to the spiritual impoverishment of everyone.

Although they are still few in number, blacks in the United States are found in white institutions of higher education. Some of these are places that were limited and perhaps closed to them prior to the civil rights movement. But most of the changes were inadequate in that they remain middle-class gains. They were inadequate in that the basic structure of economic inequality remains and helps to create what Cornel West called rootless, dangling people with few links to the supportive networks that help to sustain some sense of purpose in life. As we have seen, these gains cannot be called victories, and race discrimination still exists for those who have made it.

The achievements of the civil rights movement were subject to the rise and fall of the labor market and to the changing tides of American racism and capitalism. Still, today African Americans are disproportionately numbered among the poor, victims of violence, the unemployed, homeless, and hungry. Still, we are overrepresented in jails, prisons, single-parent families, and welfare rolls. And some perceive that a pervasive sense of despair is deepening.

If it is true that the changes in society wrought by the civil rights movement mainly benefited those few who were ready and able to take advantage once the doors of opportunity opened, then this means that the struggle for the humanization and transformation of the large river system must continue. It needs the ongoing work, the struggle, and imaginative efforts of each generation to expand and fulfill the work of societal transformation. Dr. Vincent Harding, a close associate of Dr. Martin Luther King Jr., said:

> I think we need to pay great attention to the changes that took place in the spirit and attitudes of individuals and communities, especially in the south. I saw some very deep changes, and I heard testimony to many more as men and women from every strata found their voices and caught a hint of their capacities to challenge the status quo, the ancient order. Unfortunately, most of the northern Black communities did not experience this change, but many Black southerners did. If we discount this inner transformation are we giving in to a materialist understanding of what is important in social change?[13]

A materialist reading of social change would trivialize or ignore the fact that inner, spiritual transformation is an inseparable part of social transformation. The ongoing struggle for social transformation must touch the spirit and attitudes of individuals as well as humanize the workings of social institutions. Can these ideals be taught or caught in the family? Can they be taught or caught in therapy?

Left behind in the mid-century's civil rights struggle were the truly disadvantaged. They were found primarily in inner-city neighborhoods. Many were also the forgotten rural poor. William Julius Wilson described the truly disadvantaged as comprising one of the most serious domestic problems facing the United States. He describes the problems of deteriorating schools, housing, and common infrastructure, along with a diminished tax base. This is further complicated by a self-perpetuating cycle of joblessness, teenage pregnancies, out-of-wedlock births, female-headed families, welfare dependency, and serious crime, which leads to frustration, despair, violence, and early death.[14]

This self-perpetuating cycle may be erroneously attributed to individuals or groups. When this is done, attention is diverted from the silent workings of the large river system and placed on those who are being pulled under. This self-perpetuating cycle in the land of freedom is a function of American society. The undercurrents of this large river system draw an increasing number of its citizens into the ranks of a permanent marginalized group. They are among the ones that social scientists have focused on within the past few decades.

How are we to understand the shaping of our spiritual lives in the large river system? The theologian, philosopher, and cultural analyst Cornel West has suggested that a pervasive spiritual impoverishment is growing in black America. It is related to a collapse of meaning in life, the eclipse of hope and absence of love, and the breakdown of family and neighborhood bonds.[15] But is this sense of "pervasive spiritual impoverishment" limited to black America? Indeed, it reflects a pervasive malaise at the heart of U.S. society and the seeming inability of American institutions to sustain hope and generate new meaning for an increasing number of Americans. This includes a growing number of white people. If this is the case, then we need to think long and hard about the direction of "the mainstream." Is the mainstream leading us further toward "spiritual impoverishment, collapse of meaning in life . . . the eclipse of hope . . . the absence of love of self and others, the breakdown of family, and neighborhood bonds?" Was the bombing of a federal building in Oklahoma City by one who faithfully served in the Gulf War a symbol of white American discontent? Was the Unabomber another symbol of white disillusionment? Does the Unabomber's criticism of the direction of U.S. society have any merit, or can he easily be dismissed as an antisocial, eccentric terrorist and public enemy number one? Perhaps such people represent only the tip of an iceberg; the major portion of American discontent may still be invisible. What ought to be the direction of the mainstream? Is it our calling to simply go with the flow and uncritically enter into full participation in *this* mainstream? Or are we called to challenge it, to remake it, to create new rivers, new streams? To choose the former is to deepen the spiritual impoverishment of which Cornel West warns. To choose the latter is to struggle together until a new spirit comes and enables us to carve a new channel to the sea.

If therapy is oriented to help remove obstacles to growth, then the questions I try to address are these: *How can African American individuals and families find strength within themselves and within their relations? How can they help deepen life's meaning as they continue the struggle that contributes to the humanization of institutions and further contribute toward the transformation of the mainstream?* Barbara Lerner's work, to be discussed in this chapter, suggests some possibilities and implies that political empowerment through strenuous personal engagement is essential to transforming personal disintegration and political impotence. Vincent Harding observed this ideal of political empowerment through strenuous personal engagement in the Southern freedom struggle. Subjugated women and men found a source of new personal integration as they participated in an empowering social/political movement with others.[16]

The follow-up question is this: *Amidst a rising tide of violence and despair how can reflexivity and a sense of agency aid a deepening of meaning in life?* I suggest three concepts that lie at the heart of effective therapeutic and pastoral work with African American families. They are reflexivity, sense of agency, and depth of meaning. These are crucial for navigating the deep river of African American spirituality. I use the term "reflexivity" to indicate the turning back of our reflective attention on lived experience; the drawing of beneficial lessons from whatever has been done, and the creation of imaginary or anticipated outcomes. Reflexive or critical thought can help to expose, disclose, and aid in the reinterpretation of our past. It includes the willingness to struggle with contradictions and the unknown, and the hope that new possibilities may be formed that open the ways to positive social transformation. Reflexivity may conjure up unconventional images as well as traditional ones and lead to new ideas about practical solutions that project beyond current impasses toward a new future.

By "sense of agency," I mean a belief in the ability to make decisions and act on them, to resist, create anew, or otherwise exercise power to influence how things will turn out. Depth of meaning emerges as individuals learn from suffering, nurture their relationships, contribute to the growth of self and others, and mature together in wisdom and compassion. Reflexivity and a sense of agency play a vital role in finding or developing new purposes, which in turn may deepen the meaning of life.

To what extent are such ideas already represented in the mental health literature that focuses on spiritual work with African Americans? What follows is a branching off of the river to the selected literature that addresses my concerns. I track connections between spirituality, the work of the therapist, the workings of the American mainstream, and sources of hope. Although I have departed from the mainstream, I hope the reader will return to it enriched.

My guiding question is, How can we African Americans find strength within ourselves, deepen life's meaning, and potentially reorder the life of our larger institutions? How can information derived from this question be helpful to family therapists or pastoral caregivers as well as to families themselves? Therapists, African American churches, and families have, in various ways, responded to the eclipse of hope and breakdown of supportive family bonds and networks in African American neighborhoods. Their contributions will be selectively assessed, since they work to guide, support, and facilitate healing processes within family relations.

Barbara Lerner's book is such a guide. In 1972, the results of her five-year research on outpatient psychotherapy—with nontraditional clients who were severely disturbed, or lower-class, or both—were published. Her book, *Therapy in the Ghetto: Political Impotence and Personal Disintegration,* had a profound effect on my thinking and practice as a therapist. She stated in research terms what I had experienced as a politically active pastoral therapist who worked in the inner city. Lerner's central point was that personal disintegration and related psychosocial problems are functions of political impotence. Personal disintegration results from cumulative experiences of isolation, rejection, unilateral decision making experienced as imposed power, and hostility from professional mental and medical health workers and other decision makers in one's own community. The negative effects of these cumulative experiences amplify one another. Lerner argued that there was and continues to be strong evidence for rejecting psychotherapy as a resource relevant to the mental health of lower-class urban dwellers. For many reasons, despair and hopelessness appear to be "concentrated among the poor, and the poor tend to be concentrated in particular geographical areas."[17] In such geographical areas mental health services such as psychotherapy tend to be either sorely lacking or offered by inexperienced or untrained therapists.[18] The poor in America, whom Lerner refers to, include impoverished blacks in urban ghettos, Appalachian whites, American Indians, Southeast Asians, Puerto Ricans, and Mexican Americans. They are a diverse group and comprise a marginalized group with diverse needs. Lerner's main focus is low-income and/or poor blacks. She was keen to point out that the basic problem facing them emanates from the workings of social institutions, the economic and political systems of American society. Lerner argued:

> The best evidence we have indicates that . . . the social pathology of the society in which ghetto dwellers live is the basic problem and gives rise to the personal difficulties with which they struggle. In such settings, treating "patients" without attempting to modify the social conditions which produce them is a Sisyphus-like task, somewhat analogous to treating malaria victims in a mosquito-infested swamp. Treating those already afflicted is a humane, even a heroic endeavor, but a rather futile one unless there is a simultaneous effort to drain the swamps to prevent new infections.[19]

Lerner believed that psychotherapy is a better form of treatment for individuals from deprived social environments *when it is part of a larger effort of primary prevention aimed at changing social conditions*. This approach is most effective when it includes the participation of individuals in their own social recovery. In this way individuals can engage in a reflexive social process that brings greater self-awareness into contexts of social change. This facilitates a sense of moral agency. Lerner used the terms "therapeutic community" and "participatory democracy" to spell out her vision of hope. When individuals were consulted and shared in making the decisions that directly affected their lives, their own sense of agency and psychological well-being was enhanced. As we can see, Lerner named the same set of issues that Cornel West identified 21 years later, namely, a growing sense of despair and hopelessness in black America. West used the term "nihilism" to signal that the crisis had deepened. Unfortunately, no author addresses all dimensions. Lerner did not address families, nor did she address the potentially resourceful role of religious communities, institutions, or spirituality in African Americans. Edgar H. Auerswald called attention to the important role of cognitive development. Salvador Minuchen addressed family structure and organization. Both Auerswald and Minuchen, however, ignored the religious dimension and spirituality.[20] The authors below address the role of religion and spirituality in therapeutic work with African American families.

In 1982 Barbara Ann Bass, Gail Elizabeth Wyatt, and Gloria Johnson Powell edited a volume called *The Afro-American Family: Assessment, Treatment, and Research Issues.*[21] This collection, developed over a five-year period by African American women, grew from their consultations, presentations, and interdisciplinary team approach. The articles in this edited volume center on a concern to train mental health practitioners in ethnopsychiatry and the delivery of mental health services to minority group people. The lead article by Joan E. Johnson, for example, provides a historical overview of African American family life in bondage and in freedom. "The mere survival of Africans and their descendants is phenomenal, given the infamously dehumanizing manner with which they were stripped of their rights as human beings."[22] No other group of people was brought to these shores, as a stolen people, in chains and sold as personal property on the auction block. Yet African slaves were somehow able to communicate across tribal lines and to create new cultural patterns within this large river system despite all attempts to destroy them. A key to the survival was the African's own sense of a communal self and an African kinship system. "African kinship patterns continue to influence Afro-American kinship patterns today."[23] For Johnson, the spiritual and the social-historical are woven together in traditional African sensibilities and in the experience of African American slaves.

In this same collection, Lewis M. King explored the idea that the family is the institution that perpetuates cosmological ideas of society through family rituals and rites. According to King, the way a family nurtures and perpetuates cosmological ideas—i.e., their belief in God and the order of things—is an important resource for prevention and therapeutic intervention.

Helen A. Mendes identifies "The Role of Religion in Psychotherapy with Afro-Americans." She notes that "Afro-American churches have historically played major roles in the lives of many Afro-American families."[24] Religion, however, is not confined to church, temple, or mosque goers. Mendes identifies religion broadly as including "beliefs in God, spirits, a universal law, or some other spiritual entity" held by those "who rarely, if ever, attend church."[25] Hence, there is a range and a wide variety of religious expressions to be found in African American communities. They encompass "forms of quiet meditation, genuflection, chants, whispered prayer to saints, or the forms of 'shouts,' spirit possession, and 'holy dances' done to syncopated rhythms of trumpet, drums, and tambourines."[26] Religious beliefs and values help to shape one's lifestyle and ideal self-images. They may also play an unconscious role in the psychodynamics of the treatment process. Therefore, the therapist must stay alert to the many ways religious beliefs can influence cognitive development as well as the transference and countertransference in the process of treatment.

Nancy Boyd-Franklin's comprehensive book on black families emphasizes family strengths and develops the concept of clinical empowerment and spiritual reframing.[27] Spiritual framing and reframing are a way to utilize an expressed belief such as, "God knows and will supply your every need." How does God know? How does God supply? The therapist can help family members look for ways this belief is being fulfilled in their experience. This information, when shared, may be framed in ways that can empower the family as a whole. By *empowerment* Boyd-Franklin means a therapeutic process that identifies and utilizes the family's strengths in ways that enable them to successfully interact with external systems. "Empowerment therefore consists of helping people to gain the ability to make and implement basic life decisions in their own lives and the lives of their children."[28] Religion and spirituality have been recognized as important sources of empowerment in the lives of many black people. Therefore, Boyd-Franklin encourages family therapists to explore, with sensitivity, the role that religion and spirituality plays in the lives of black clients. Boyd-Franklin identifies the importance of black churches, Jehovah's Witnesses, and the Nation of Islam and other sects. She draws certain implications of families' religious values for family therapy. Finally, she identifies four ways in which religious values and the resources of churches can be used to empower black people. They are:

> involving a minister as a consultant, co-therapist, or integral part of the treatment process; mobilizing the resources of a black church network to help a family in crisis; utilizing church networks as a support for a family during times of illness, death, or loss; and, helping isolated black families who are cut off from their original networks to create or recreate new ones.[29]

The African American pastoral theologian Romney M. Moseley was concerned with spirituality and cognitive development. He demonstrated the use of reflexivity when he focused attention on how one becomes a self before God. He demonstrated how faith and meaning in life undergo critical transformations when one is faced with life's overwhelming contradictions. Moseley identified two postures toward life, two ways a Christian might respond to life's contradictions. To oversimplify, one way is to neutralize the contradiction in life through a recognition that it is impossible to perform all of the moral duties with which the self is confronted.[30] Hence, one surrenders to God, believing that God accepts us, imperfect as we are. The other way is to approach the contradictions of life and find meaning through acts of self-giving and through solidarity with others, especially the oppressed. This is not an individual act of self-sacrifice. Rather, it is a radical commitment to build up a new kind of community through repeated acts of self-giving. Such acts join with the acts of others. Together they form streams of transformation. The challenge that Moseley points to is the ongoing transformation of everyday existence through acts of love and justice. Following the lead of Søren Kierkegaard, Moseley uses the term "repetition," the faithful reenactment of love and justice as ways to transform despair. Moseley worked out his ideas broadly and in relation to Christian liberation praxis. Unlike Barbara Lerner, his focus was not clinical work or family therapy with African American families. However, his ideas could be fruitfully applied to clinical work with African American families.

Edward P. and Anne S. Wimberly, have pioneered in the field of African American pastoral care (1979, 1982, 1986, 1990, 1991). Their valuable work has been aimed at strengthening the local congregation and pastor's use of Christian and African American resources in the provision of adequate pastoral care. In these works, the Wimberlys focus on what goes on *within* the counseling process. Their goals are to use African American spiritual resources to facilitate counseling, to evoke ideas, feelings, and attitudes, and to attend to interpersonal relationships throughout the life cycle. This is an important therapeutic focus. When such a focus is limited to technique, then the strategies needed to challenge and help transform the dominant social patterns that underlie human suffering go unnoticed. The Wimberlys, however, avoid this temptation to focus on technique because of their concern to link counseling strategies to the wider social system.

The above-mentioned authors work within the mainstream of American society. They link family problems to the workings of society. They make significant contributions to our understandings of the role of psychotherapy in low-income communities (Lerner), religious experience (Moseley), and the roles of historical interpretation, religious beliefs, family dynamics and their implications for family therapy. However, the above-mentioned therapists do not address the direction of the mainstream or its transformation. As mainstream workers, they link present-day problems to the pilgrimage from slavery (Johnson), and show the important role of kinship networks in sustaining African American families (J. Johnson, Boyd-Franklin). They show that cosmological ideas (L. M. King), religious belief and spirituality (Mendes; Boyd-Franklin) have been neglected by mental health practitioners. They also suggest the important link between spirituality and cognitive development in African American religious experience. Therapists do not have to subscribe to the same set of beliefs the family holds, but they do need to respect the manner in which religious beliefs have become meaningful to family members. What we become painfully aware of is that the workings of the mainstream also condition the thinking and strategies of the therapist and pastoral caregiver. Here the branch of the river returns to the mainstream.

In this light, *How can African American individuals and families find strength within themselves and in their relations to deepen life's meaning as they continue to struggle in a society that once enslaved and continues to isolate them? How can they participate in a way that humanizes institutions and continue struggling for the transformation of the mainstream? Amidst a rising tide of violence and despair how can reflexivity and a sense of agency aid the deepening of meaning in life and help us to reorder our institutional life?* The mainstream with its materialistic and utilitarian values is a central part of the problem we must address on the path to any reordering of our personal and institutional lives. It is, therefore, necessary to interpret personal and family difficulties in the light of an interpretation of how United States society as a whole works. It is the workings of this mainstream as a whole and our responses to it that give meaning to our experience. The deepening of meaning or purpose in life is the goal. Deepening of meaning requires the tapping of spiritual resources such as Helen Mendes, Lewis King, Nancy Boyd-Franklin, Romney Moseley, and E. P. and Anne Wimberly have indicated.

The task of this chapter was to view African American families with reference to the mainstream of American society. The American mainstream was identified as the people, traditions, social forces and institutions, beliefs and practices shaping American society. I asked, what *is* the current direction of this mainstream, and *what does it need to become?* In this light, I asked how therapists and pastoral counselors are to understand the ideological currents shaping American institutions, society's impact upon families in general, and African American families in particular. The workings of society, especially its economic system, significantly shape family structure. I used imagination, called on the work of critical thinkers, and demonstrated, through the lens of the civil rights struggle, Negro and black history, how the workings of society conditioned experience, thought, and action. This included experiences of struggle and hope, of spiritual impoverishment and despair, a sense of agency, and interpersonal choices. If a sense of spiritual impoverishment is pervasive and growing, then we are in trouble, and therapists cannot simply go with the flow. It is not enough to simply be adjusted to the large river system of American society. There is a need to raise our level of awareness about the complex nature of our ongoing struggle to humanize and help transform the larger river system as a whole. I argued that historically, spirituality has been the greatest resource for African Americans in times of trouble. Therefore, therapy cannot be divorced from the spirituality of African Americans. It is a resource to be tapped. But what happens when the church, the spiritual face of the community, is perceived as part of the problem and some members of the community no longer feel welcome there? They become spiritual refugees. In the next chapter we consider the situation of the spiritual refugee.

~

3

> *By the rivers of Babylon—*
> *there we sat down*
> *there we wept when we remembered Zion.*
>
> Psalm 137:1

> *I came to the exiles at Tel-Abib, who lived by the*
> *River Chebar. And I sat there among them, stunned,*
> *for seven days.*
>
> Ezekiel 3:15

Spiritual Refuges

The purpose of this chapter is to address the question of how to relate to a growing number of spiritually disillusioned, yet spiritually hungry, African Americans whose spiritual needs and questions are not addressed by secular society or by black church religious cultures. I shall argue that on the one hand, spiritual refugees represent a relatively new and emerging group of disenchanted African Americans who may find common cause with others who are fugitives from their customary place of worship in an increasingly secular society. They pose an important challenge for therapists. On the other hand, African American spiritual refugees are not new.

35

Africans, uprooted from the land of their ancestors and enslaved in America, came to these shores as spiritual refugees and had to improvise spiritual resources in a hostile environment. They became "the endless flow of black fugitives" as they fled persecution in the southern United States and sought refuge in the North, Canada, Cuba, or elsewhere.[1] They forged new ways to worship the God who struggled with them for freedom.

Who is the spiritual refugee? Ours is a secular society where God has been edged out. Therefore, the wider context for appreciating this concept of "spiritual refugee" is the mainstream of American society. In this chapter, we consider the question, Who is the refugee? There is no single definition of refugee that is suitable for all purposes. But there are certain common characteristics that refugees share. These are: being uprooted, homeless, and landless; seeking shelter in another place; losing the protection of one's rights; imprisonment; and deportation. The term "refugee" comes to mind when descriptions of human experience include the terms *driven out, persecuted, flight, homeless, shunned, condemned,* and *culturally isolated.* "Refugee" is used in this chapter to describe persons who have experienced persecution and have been uprooted from their home church. They seek refuge somewhere.

A 17-year-old Ghanian girl, Fauziya, fled her native country for the United States when she became betrothed to a 45-year-old man whom she had never met. Her father did not believe in polygamy, forced marriage, or female circumcision. He educated his five daughters to share those beliefs. When he died, Fauziya was 17, and things suddenly changed. The father's sister, according to tribal rules, inherited her deceased brother's home, banished the wife, ended Fauziya's schooling and betrothed her to a 45-year-old man whom she had never met. This meant that she was scheduled for ritual female mutilation and would be one of several wives. Before this could happen, Fauziya fled to the United States with the help of a family member. She had plans to stay with relatives. When she arrived at U.S. immigration, she was treated like a criminal, handcuffed, and sent to prison because an immigration judge did not believe her story. Eventually, Fauziya was granted refugee status.[2] I use the term "refugee" as analogous to those who have been uprooted or have left their spiritual home in search of a new one, generally because they have been persecuted. They seek refuge from persecution in another place and are in need of security, safety, and comfort.

Who, then, is the "spiritual" refugee? The spiritual refugee is the person driven out from his or her customary place of worship by persecution and made "homeless." Such persons cannot return to their former places of spiritual nurture. This experience is analogous to that of the political refugee. Spiritual refugees have been rejected, traumatized, or ousted by powerful forces that operate in church and society. Their rights are not protected. These experiences have been internalized and may be manifested in a sense of lowered self-esteem, depression and outrage, disorientation, anxiety, and loneliness. The spiritual refugee experiences a profound sense of distrust and has not yet found a new and secure place to be. Yet these are sensitive souls, moved by deep and true religious questions and longings. To whom can they turn? Who can provide a secure base for an exploration of their spiritual quest, longings, and options? How can their spiritual striving be understood, respected, framed or reframed? Are there any general norms or universal principles that can guide the work of the caregiver who works with the spiritual refugee? When does the spiritual refugee cease being a spiritual refugee? Who decides, and how is it decided?

Near the end of his seminary training, a student who had successfully defended his M.A. thesis told me that he was "leaving the Church behind."

> Simply put, I am finding myself caring less and less about "theology" of any kind. To put it more bluntly, my investment in the "Christian Religious Community" is pretty nonexistent.
>
> "Nonexistent" strikes me as rather a harsh word for someone who is just receiving his master's degree from a seminary, yet it has the ring of truth for me. It is truth because it reflects some major decisions (both conscious and not) to pull away from the Church and live my life, if not in opposition to it, at least away from it. . . . Trusting relationships, be they with individuals in a church, significant clergy persons, or one's own relationship to "God-language" and rituals, must be mutually nurtured and developed. Mine were consistently not.

This was said by a student who had invested in the life of the church. He felt uprooted by hate and no longer welcomed in the church, which once was his spiritual home. Paradoxically, he still felt "emotionally identified" with the church. He left the church behind and took refuge in opposing its homophobic attitudes and practices because he felt persecuted by it. This student was a member of a minority group, self-aware, sensitive to injustices, outspoken and courageous.

His is not a lone voice. He is part of a growing group of disillusioned and disaffiliated Christians. He was not African American, but his experience of persecution and rejection, flight from the church, and opposing it resonate with the experiences of some African Americans.

Many African Americans have been oppressed by and driven from traditional black churches because of their homophobic teachings and seeming inability to face the entire issue of human sexuality creatively. A black Christian lesbian said:

> The African American community has been damaged by teachings of the Church that homosexuality is a dysfunction. The Church's homophobic stance and negative teachings have driven some to suicide and others to leading closeted double lives. These negative teachings have rendered too many African American gay and lesbian youth homeless and the objects of horrendous violent crimes. The problem is the collateral damage experienced by all African Americans who are diminished by homophobia, and open lesbians and gays who are condemned and culturally isolated by the church and shunned by the community.[3]

Gays and lesbians are among the spiritual refugees, but they are not the only ones. There are many others who flee the institutional African American church. Some are pregnant teenagers who have been ostracized. Others have been driven out because of ongoing internecine power conflicts. Others have left because of sexual and/or spiritual abuse. Still others leave for theological reasons and believe that the church is resistant to change, openness, and newness. They have decided to take responsibility for their own spiritual lives.[4] Materialism and the secular spirit of society generate broader influences.

Secular Society as Contemporary Context

Secular society is the wider context for evaluating the spiritual refugee experience. The relatively recent interest in spirituality is in part a response to a modern secular society that fails to nurture spiritual needs and denies the central importance of religious faith and transcending values. The operation of Western secular society contributes to the creation of the spiritual refugee by generating conditions that disrupt community attachments and sweep away the supports for religious beliefs, thereby leaving many people, not just African Americans, spiritually uprooted. Everyone is affected by the way the mainstream operates. The situation of spiritually disillusioned African Americans is the tip of the iceberg. It is part of a deeper malaise operating in Western cultures that separate the spiritual dimension from its technical and practical interests. While the focus here is on African Americans, the problem of the spiritual refugee is a general twentieth-century one. Everyone is affected in some way by the profound changes created, in part, by the cultural, societal, and political upheavals of our time. Secular society and its processes of modernization, bureaucratic organization, technological communication, and demographic shifts has contributed to the disintegration of traditional forms of living. Under these conditions social ties and cultural traditions have ceased to provide security. Religious truths have been doubted or abandoned. The family and self have become more vulnerable to breakdown. As a consequence family life and individual experience undergo significant transformation as people search for new identities in their quest to make sense of their experiences. Personal experiences in secular society are marked by rapid change, anxiety and stress, discontinuity, dislocation, and fragmentation.

I see this phenomenon as a conditioning influence on contemporary spiritual experience, of which African American experience is a part. I see the experiences of spiritual refugees as providing a part of the challenge for transforming and humanizing the social mainstream when their experiences are taken seriously—i.e., when their stories and metaphors are encouraged and serve as a source of information about society, the family, and the self.

39

According to Anthony Elliot, life in secular society engenders our deepest hopes and fears. Secular society "multiplies, dislocates, and disperses the psychological forms of everyday reality. It destroys modern structures of time, space, history, and truth, and replaces them with a celebration and pluralization of brute immediacy."[5] The underpinnings that sustain a sense of security and moral commitment contribute to the interrelatedness of family life and self-organization. They are continuously challenged, if not dismantled by the complex and contradictory working of secular society. A perverse internal logic is at work. The internal logic of our secular society breaks up social reality into chunks of experience without referents, structure, or unity.[6]

Is this the case (i.e., that a perverse internal logic is at work in secular society and only serves to fragment experience)? Perhaps this view of society is limited because it fails to consider the work of the spirit, human resiliency, and improvisation. To improvise is to create something new and spontaneously out of the resources immediately available. Improvisation may contribute to the emergence of new social networks. In Anthony Elliot's view of the world, how does one improvise and conjure hope? The student whom I quoted at the beginning of this chapter left behind a church community that he found to be alienating in order to invest in new networks or relationships that were nurturing.

Where do refugees turn and how can new meaning in life be created, sustained, and even deepened within a disorienting and secular society? What is the role of reflexivity and sense of agency amidst a growing sense of disillusionment and spiritual malaise? What inspires social activism, the transformation of old social networks, or the creation of new ones that help sustain the dogged struggle toward social transformation?

Needed are a point of reference and recognition of spiritual resources for conjuring hope. Alternative communities form because of the experiences of dislocation and alienation. People seek refuge in alternative communities in order to counter the alienating effects of society and restore a sense of security, connection, and intimacy with others and the Divine. Groups who have experienced dislocation and persecution include the Mormons, who fled to Utah in the nineteenth century; Women Church, Universal Fellowship of Metropolitan Community Church (UFMCC); and other kinds of collectives formed in the late twentieth century. These were and are communities responding to modern social oppression and engaged in building alternative communities.

In alternative communities people are able to find psychological and spiritual support, and moral grounds for their activities. In such alternative communities it is possible for refugees to reenvision themselves as coparticipants in a contemporary struggle to humanize social order and to augment their inner reserves through communal support. What do family therapists and pastoral caregivers need to know, be, and learn about using reflexivity and a sense of agency in order to help transform old networks or help to create new ones in efforts to deepen meaning in life and meet the needs of the spiritual refugee who no longer affiliates with black church cultures?

Several white therapists and colleagues have shared that some of those spiritual refugees are turning to them for therapy and refuge. They do not want to be seen by an African American therapist. They report being alienated from the church and are looking for alternative expressions of spirituality. Because they have turned to the white therapist for refuge does not mean they have been successful in leaving the church behind. They may still have deep attachments to the church, even if they cannot return to it. It is important for the therapist to explore deep-rooted and unresolved spiritual issues by being alert to the language, images, and metaphors used to describe one's existential experiences. The deep river of African American spirituality in which they have been immersed will remain wherever they go. Therefore, this turn to certain therapists may prove to be a challenge. Therapists who have been trained in the mainstream of mental health disciplines have learned to conceive of and measure human functioning separate from a consideration of religious and spiritual values. Indeed, they have learned to regard spirituality as private. They may share a popular view of African American spirituality as overly emotional, complacent, and anti-intellectual. Therefore, they may be suspicious of African American spirituality. Black psychologist and musician Arthur C. Jones argued that the popular conceptions of spirituality encourage a "primarily individualist, private form of spiritual practices" that inhibits social responsibility and the confronting of oppressive power arrangements. Therapists tend to emphasize inner or individualistic approaches to spirituality and may "fail to understand the unlimited potential of communal sharing as a facilitator of individual growth."[7]

If this is the case, then it is important for therapists, especially secular therapists, to understand the importance of African American culture and the influence of the church in both its affirming and disaffirming functions. The church has been affirming when it has nurtured the devotees' relationship to the Divine, fostered self-worth in the presence of others, and strengthened a sense of love and justice in relationships. It has been disaffirming when it has shunned the pregnant teenager or young unwed mother, promoted or justified oppression, especially the oppression of gays and lesbians, women and children—i.e., treating wives or women and children as servants of men. These influences are in tension with the call for inclusion and wider justice in black churches. The radical call is toward the full humanity of all persons, young single mothers, gays and lesbians, women, children, and men. Ignorance of these tensions and multiple (and often contradictory) influences will limit the therapist's effectiveness. In this light, a colleague asked if psychoanalytic training, with its generally pejorative orientation toward religion, disqualifies a therapist from working with spiritual refugees. The answer to this question depends on what therapists are willing to unlearn and learn afresh from the evolving experiences and cultures that are different from their own and are considered to be marginal to the American mainstream. To recognize the influence of African American culture and church is to draw on a history of continuing struggle, where spiritual refugees may be harbingers of something new and are frequently challenged to negotiate hope in the midst of despair. In this light and in societies influenced by Christianity, biblical images become natural carriers of a people's struggles and hope, as expressed, for example, in black spirituals, gospel songs, the blues, or proverbs.[8] Therefore, secular therapists need to know that African American

42

spirituality continues to evolve and that African Americans are a spiritual people who frequently use biblical language or imagery whether they define themselves as religious (i.e., practicing, or churchgoing) or not.

Slavery as Original Context

The original matrix for African American spiritual refugees was the experience of being uprooted from one's homeland and transported thousands of miles away to a new world as a slave. Slave religion was the particular institution that sustained the slave and in which the slave took refuge. At the heart of slave religion was the yearning to be free from bondage. This yearning found expression in rebellions as well as in songs, dance, ritual practices, and prayer traditions. These helped to bind the slave community together and enabled them to resist, endure, and imaginatively transform themselves and their world. At the heart of their religion was "The Book," the Bible, which told them they were God's people and offered supporting images. As Arthur C. Jones informs us in *Wade in the Water,* those supporting images were translated into spirituals and became a source of internal grounding and motivation of external action.[9] "The Book" helped to shape their active faith and revolutionary struggle for social justice. When freedom was a long way off, the Bible helped to sustain their hope that someday they would be free. The day of freedom was just around the bend. It was this view of the future that pulled them forward in their bleakest hour. At the center of African American spirituality is the yearning to be free and related, along with the capacity to live in the world as it is while projecting beyond it toward a world that is yet to be.

The Bible has been a primary source for sustenance in present troubles while projecting beyond them. It is a source for social criticism and personal correction. It has inspired social activism. It has been a visionary source for conjuring social transformation. In this light, therapists can learn to conjure the past as a reference point for hope in the present. The mechanism for emotional, physical, and spiritual survival and resistance often emerges under conditions of threat, and in ways that enable an oppressed group to rise above their oppressors and envision their liberation.[10] For example,

African American religious experience has been interpreted in the light of the story of ancient Israel, where a people were enslaved, carried into captivity, and wept as they sat by the rivers of Babylon. They became refugees, and moved forward toward a vision of a land promised by God.

Theophus H. Smith, in an unusual interdisciplinary work, *Conjuring Culture,* identifies the central role of the Bible in conjuring in African American spirituality and religious experience.[11] He joins biblical imagery with an interest in historical transformation and with therapeutic intent. Interest in biblical and other literary sources of imagery informs the social imagination and political activism of African Americans. Smith employs an unconventional definition of "conjure," which includes healing as well as cursing by magical means.

Conjuring culture, then, is not only a way to interpret what is going on, it is also a way to transform reality. The term "conjure," he argues, means "magic." It is "best understood as one system, among humanity's more primal cognitive systems, for mapping and managing the world in the form of signs."[12] It is an enduring system of communication and has three interrelated meanings: "(1) to invoke or summon (up) a spirit, as in sorcery; (2) to effect by the use of 'magical' arts; and finally (3) to summon up an image or an idea as an act of imagination."[13] As an interpreter of African American and Western religious cultures, Smith further understands conjure as "a pharmacopeic tradition of practices"[14] that can call up both healing and harm. Both therapeutic (or curative) and harmful elements are central to conjuring in African American culture. "I refer to such transformations as instances of conjuring culture, specifically where I find (1) ritually patterned behaviors and performative uses of language and symbols, (2) conveying a pharmacopeic or healing/harming intent, and (3) employing biblical figures and issuing in biblical configurations of cultural experience."[15]

Smith expands a description of "conjure" to include curative transformations of reality by means of imitation or by mimetic operations and processes.[16] This point becomes crucial for our direction in that the present configuration of the world is provisional. The world as we know it yields to the passage of time. It is passing away, but at the same time it is constantly imbued with transformative possibilities through repetition and creative activity. Through imitation, symbolic performances, and reenactment of the biblical narratives, one is able to see how God is purposefully at work in the social world as its creative ground. This perspective of the provisional character of the world as a place for God's purposeful activity is missing from Anthony Elliot's view of the world's "perverse internal logic" and "brute immediacy."

Through this description of conjuring, Smith identifies the Bible as a conjure book, which African Americans use to interpret and reinterpret their experience of healing and curse, and to envision a transformed future. In this way, African Americans may employ biblical imagery to augment their inner reserves, envision themselves as coparticipants in a contemporary struggle to humanize the social order and create bonds of inclusion based on love, power, and justice. Smith uses conjure as practice and as a root metaphor for ritual, figural, and therapeutic transformations of African American culture and spirituality. How can this information help the therapist to think constructively about the use of a sacred text, and the goals, aims, or objectives of therapy?

There are many ways to state the goals of therapeutic activity. One way is to seek to restore the person not only to a sense of balance but also to a sense of connection or cultural relatedness within a caring relationship and transforming community. Therapists might ask, How can the help seeker learn to contribute toward the creation of the secure kind of community she or he desires? Conjuring such a possibility is critical to an envisioning of therapeutic goals. If conjuring is one of many primal cognitive sign systems for mapping and transforming reality, then what cognitive systems do caregivers use to understand the present and envision the future with spiritual refugees? The strong suggestion here is that the Bible and biblical narratives are among the significant resources for understanding and interpreting the symbolic universe of African American spiritual refugees. To improvise on biblical material and make it relevant to African Americans is a part of the African American's spiritual legacy. Arthur C. Jones makes this point:

> The ability of Africans in bondage to utilize biblical material functionally, as an integral feature of their daily spiritual and community life is . . . related to their facility with improvisation,

which is another prominent feature of the African tradition. Not only were early African Americans able to improvise on biblical material to make it relevant to their own needs, but they were able as well to employ material from various songs and biblical stories in infinite combinations and permutations, continually creating new versions of already existing songs. This reflected their spontaneous ability to improvise in a manner consistent with the needs of specific circumstances.[17]

Perhaps this manner of working with spiritual refugees has the potential to transform and enlarge our understanding of therapy. If African American culture is rooted in African religious traditions and is often interpreted through biblical imagery, then some familiarity with or curiosity about this imagery by therapists is indispensable to an interpretation of the African American refugee experience. The temptation for the therapist trained in Western psychology is to view the spiritual refugee individually and separate from collective experience—as if the individual psychic experience could be adequately understood separate from collective experience.

Where scripture is important in the life of the counselee, its appropriate use will be important in the context of therapy. This means that therapists need to be curious about and develop ways to combine knowledge of scripture or sacred text with skillful therapeutic application. Some counselees may not know, right away, the important role that Scripture can play or has played in their lives. I once heard a young African American woman passionately say that for a long time she lived by the faith of her mother and grandmother. She had never really made the faith her own until her life became deeply troubled. She felt empty. "I did not know God for myself," she said. It was then that she recognized that she was living a faith borrowed from her mother and grandmother. Her faith was shallow. She was not grounded in the faith or in the sacred literature and practices that could inform and help to deepen the channels of her faith and action. She did not know how important Scripture could be in her life until troubles came. Through anguished searching and struggle she finally came to know God for herself. She then quoted a familiar spiritual: "It's not my mother, nor my brother, but it's me, O Lord, standing in the need of prayer!"

Many African Americans, young and old, have been uprooted from their familiar places of worship (for various reasons) and have left the church behind. They have left it behind because the church had become a place of oppression and no longer fed them spiritually. Some have come to the therapist's office, a riverbank, a place to reflect and to recollect. The therapist, then, needs to be curious about how experience and spiritual traditions have shaped each other. Therapists can become curious about the way their counselees relate spiritual resources to their troubles. What resources, metaphors, and images do they employ? How can these be enriched or revised? Therapists can help make sense of the spiritual traditions that have given support in past struggles. They can help with the interpretation of Scripture or sacred texts that now need to be revisited and reexamined in the light of the spiritual refugee's valid and emerging experience. How can Scripture or sacred texts be reappropriated and their meaning deepened in the life of the spiritual refugee? How can internal spiritual reserves be augmented? If the therapist shows a lack of interest in the texts that have informed the life of the spiritual refugee, then the therapist may not be able to help with the reinterpretation of this part of the spiritual refugee's experience.

Scripture as Resource

Below, I select a passage of Scripture as an example of a biblical text that might be relevant to the therapist's work with spiritual refugees. The Scripture is about the experience of being uprooted (Psalm 137:1–9).

> By the rivers of Babylon—there we sat down;
> and there we wept when we remembered Zion.
> On the willows there
> we hung up our harps.
> For there our captors asked us for songs;
> and our tormentors asked for mirth, saying,
> "Sing us one of the songs of Zion!"
> How could we sing the Lord's song
> in a foreign land?

If I forget you, O Jerusalem,
let my right hand wither!
Let my tongue cling to the roof of my mouth,
if I do not remember you,
if I do not set Jerusalem above my highest joy.
    Remember, O Lord, against the Edomites
the day of Jerusalem's fall, how they said,
"Tear it down! Tear it down! Down to its foundations!"
O daughter Babylon, you devastator!
Happy shall they be who pay you back
what you have done to us!
Happy shall they be who take your little ones
and dash them against the rock!

This is a sorrow song of a people uprooted and carried off into captivity by their tormentors. The song shows us the important role of memories of pain and emotional expression, nurture and resistance when one is uprooted. Memories also invoke or summon up a spirit that provides the anchor, a secure base that enables the uprooted ones to endure. It may stimulate awareness of new resources or awareness of how resources may be fashioned anew. By the rivers of Babylon, what was sacred and under protection is now trivialized. Their captors trivialize their faith and torment them. They torment by asking them to share, for entertainment, what is most precious to them, their sacred songs. They respond with a rhetorical question: How can they sing the song of their Lord in a foreign place? Place is so important to the uprooted ones. When one is violently uprooted from one's secure place, then there is a sense in which even their sacred songs are not available, "How can we sing the Lord's song in a foreign land?" What they have, then, is memory of the former place, Jerusalem, the place of security and nurture. This place is so important for the centering of the spiritual life that the uprooted ones are even willing to call down a curse upon themselves, "If I forget you, O Jerusalem, let my right hand wither!" The psalmist uses a negative self-reference to express a positive devotion to Jerusalem ("if I forget . . .") and a positive blessing to express negative feeling of retribution toward Babylon ("Happy the ones who . . .") There is the note of revenge that the uprooted ones call to mind. They remember the destruction that was called on their sacred place, "Tear it down! "Tear it down!" And they yearn for retributive justice. African Americans are vitally interested in issues of retributive justice and reparation.

African Americans have been able to make this psalm their song when they remember their collective experience of uprootedness from their homeland. Our history resonates with the history of ancient Israel. "As we have seen, Africans in America were able to extend themselves backward and forward in history, utilizing biblical accounts of past events to relate to both current realities and expectations of future events."[18] When the psalmist called upon the spiritual resources that lie deep within, he or she was doing the work that every spiritual refugee must do, to remember what gives security, to anticipate the possibility that one's former sense of security will be trivialized or ridiculed, to name the place and traditions that bring nurture, to mourn, and to express the rage that accompanies the experience of being uprooted.

The psalm begins with the important words, "By the rivers of Babylon." The riverbank was the place of rest and reflection. It was there that they sat down. It was there that they wept. It was there that they could recollect. But even there, they were vulnerable to the taunts of their captors. Even then, their resistance was greatest because the riverbank of experience provided the opportunity to recollect. The exilic prophet, Ezekiel, visited the captives by the River Chebar "and for seven days I stayed there, overcome by what I had seen and heard" (Ezekiel 3:15b).

How, then, can this passage of Scripture help or instruct the caregiver who works with the spiritual refugee? There are at least two ways:

1. In times of trouble, African Americans have been strongest and most hopeful whenever they have been able to conjure up the past as backdrop for the struggle of the present. Their history and spiritual legacy is the riverbank that provides models for nurture and sustenance when all hope appears to be gone. At times such as these it is vitally important to invoke or summon (up) appropriate images that strengthen a sense of connection with others, give hope, and encourage a sense of agency.

2. They may be helped to know that both healing *and* curse operate together. Pain and a sense of revenge, nurture and resistance, are linked and must be summoned. The psalmist reaches out for healing memories and at the same time recites the horrible things that were done, and calls down a curse on those who oppress. The psalm reminds us that the opportunity to express the range of all of these emotions from rage to joy, on the riverbank, are part of the work that the spiritual refugee must do, and this work is integral to personal and social transformation.

Tapping Spiritual Resources in Therapy

I share the following to illustrate how a therapist or caregiver might use self, a range of emotions, Scripture, and prayer within the context of therapy. I once worked with a devout Seventh-day Adventist mother who had left behind the church in which she grew up; she left the church her mother attends. In so doing she was leaving an unresolved and troublesome relationship with her mother. The spiritual currents moving in her life took her in a different direction. Although she had taken refuge in another church, still it did not satisfy her spiritual hunger. Dissatisfaction is a reminder that institutions and human systems are finite. They cannot completely satisfy the hunger for spiritual wholeness. One is reminded of Psalm 42:2, "My soul thirsts for God, for the living God. When shall I come and behold the face of God." St. Augustine said something similar, "Our Souls are restless until we find our Rest in Thee."

One day, she talked about her continuing conflict with her mother, difficulties at work, physical pain, sense of being overwhelmed as a single parent, and her fears. I wondered what would bring her a sense of fulfillment. If these difficulties would magically go away, would she be fulfilled? I recognized that I was limited in what I could do to help change her outer reality. I listened, encouraged her to express her inner reality, her emotions and beliefs. I asked what she had already done and what her plans were for the immediate future. I noted the images she called up as she sat by her river of Babylon and longed for a Jerusalem.

I thought that if I could help her to express what she was feeling and sharpen the image of the forces that held her captive or seemed to overwhelm her, then possibly I could help increase her sense of agency, further help her to sort out the bits and pieces of her difficulty, and conjure up images of hope. Helping people to name their captors and the manner in which they are tormented, and changing their images and pictures of reality is a part of the work of transformation. If people are able to more clearly see the bits and pieces that make up the big forces that overwhelm them, then they are in a better position to redefine their situation, make new decisions, carve a new channel for their energies, and better face the storms of life. But what resources would she draw on to accomplish this?

I was aware of her deep faith and I thought that perhaps it could become more of a resource for her. As I listened to her, several passages of Scripture came to mind, mostly from the psalms and wisdom literature—such as, "Why are you cast down, O my soul, and why are you disquieted within me? Hope in God" (Psalm 42:5). I was familiar enough with passages of Scripture that I knew how to find them quickly. Near the end of our therapy session, I shared that I felt moved by her struggle and pain, and that I felt moved to share a passage of Scripture that her words brought to mind, and to pray. She said, "I'd like that." As I read, she leaned forward and listened intently. Because of the choice of Scripture, she knew that I had been listening intently to her. She was very quiet during the brief prayer, which lifted up her struggle and her hope. At the end of the prayer, she sat quietly for a few minutes, got up, and walked out.

She called for another appointment and appeared much more hopeful than when I last saw her. Soon after that she began to talk more openly about her faith and her struggles with God and her church. She shared her complaints, disappointments, disgust, and hopes. Then one day she announced that she had been invited to preach the sermon, but she did not believe that women should preach from the pulpit. I suggested that maybe something new is happening. She told me that she wanted to preach on love and fear and asked if I knew of any passages of Scripture that would help her. I mentioned 1 John 4:18, "There is no fear in love, but perfect love cast out fear." I told her that if she wanted more, then we could find them. She was delighted and said that was the start she needed.

She told me of the day she was to preach. I asked if I could come to hear her. She expressed surprise that I would come and said yes.

Her sermon revealed a great deal of preparation. It was powerful both in content and delivery. As part of her sermon, she dramatized Sojourner Truth's famous speech, "Ain't I a Woman?!" Through this sermon and dramatization she stated her own emerging truth, faith, courage, and solidarity with others who suffer as she had.

I do not frequently make use of Scripture and prayer in the way that I did with this devout Seventh-day Adventist help seeker, who in her own way is a spiritual refugee. But I remember that when we began our counseling relationship she said that she was looking for a black, male, Christian counselor. She was specific, and I knew then that I was being given permission to include the resources of my faith in our work. The secular caregiver who is not given this permission from the outset of therapy, as I was, will need to explore throughout the course of therapy what are the inner resources the help seeker draws on in times of struggle. The help giver might ask herself or himself, "What do I need to know about the help seeker that links her or him to where they are in their life journey?" And, "What do I need to do to facilitate their spiritual growth?" The secular caregiver can be curious about the practices, proverbs, special sayings, metaphors, or other sources of inspiration the help seekers uses.

It was helpful to see her at work within the wider context of her faith community, her church family, to observe the responses others made to her and to gain deeper appreciation for her creative imagination. Her mother and daughter were in attendance at the service. After the service and after the praise of others, her mother congratulated her on a job well done. This was important.

This experience then became an added reference point for our therapeutic work. By employing biblical imagery in relation to her difficulties, a source of internal grounding and motivation for action was provided. In this way, I was able to tap into faith resources and to deepen the work of therapy in such a way that her own faith became even more of an integral part of her work both in and out of therapy.

But not everyone feels welcomed by the church, as my student signaled at the outset of this chapter. These were among his last words to me:

> The reality which the Church has created is flawed deeply. Emotionally identifying with it appears to be not only fruitless, but something of a double-bind for gay persons. I believe many les-

bians see this in a clearer manner than do many of my gay brothers who are still struggling with the pull of emotional identification and the push of sexual guilt within the Church. For me, my personal and relational health is threatened by placing myself within the structure of the Church. The choice to pull away strikes me as a wise and important step toward my human growth, continued relationship to others, and to my physical and spiritual environment.

My student died of AIDS on Thanksgiving Day 1986. He left behind an important challenge for the churches, namely, to creatively face the entire issue of human sexuality and become a more inclusive Christian community of wider justice. Spiritual refugees are those who have left or are leaving the church behind. Some are defecting in place.[19] Their numbers are increasing as the millennium comes to a close. Spiritual refugees are electing to take responsibility for their own spiritual lives. Some are turning to a therapist for refuge as they work to create an alternative spiritual environment. They are part of the transformation of church and society.

We recall the 17-year-old who fled mutilation in Ghana, her native land, to find refuge with relatives in the United States. She experienced further trauma at immigration because of ignorance. Her story was not believed and she was treated like a criminal before she was granted refugee status. She speaks for thousands of others in her situation. Her experience is also an analogy for spiritual refugees whose stories are discounted. They are the ostracized young unwed mother, women, children and men, gays and lesbians, the spiritually disillusioned, yet spiritually hungry who feel betrayed by the church. They are our brothers and sisters and children. We must prepare ourselves to listen to them and to utilize spiritual resources in the humanization of institutions, in our responses, and in the transformation of society. It is, therefore, imperative to listen to what spiritual refugees from different backgrounds are saying and how they name experiences of the human and Divine.

~

4

WE CARRY THE PAIN AND THE HOPE:
THE JOURNEY TO THE SEA

*Can a negro, whose ancestors were imported into
this country, and sold as slaves, become a member
of the political community formed and brought into
existence by the Constitution of the United States, and
as such become entitled to all the rights, and privileges, and immunities, guaranteed by that instrument
to the citizens?*

Roger Taney,
Chief Justice of the U.S. Supreme Court,
1856

*This is a country for white men, and by God so
long as I am President, it shall be a government for
white men.*

Andrew Johnson,
17th President of the United States,
1865

*When we say we will put America first, we mean
also that our Judaeo-Christian values are going to be
preserved and our Western heritage is going to be
handed down to future generations and not dumped
into some landfill called multiculturalism.*

Pat Buchanan, Presidential Candidate,
The Independent, 22 February 1996

The Power of Questions

The purpose of this chapter is to focus on the important role of questions in therapy, and in life generally. To question means to search for something that is missing (e.g., where did I put my keys?). It is an intervention that calls attention to a particular experience (e.g., keys are missing) and singles it out for special activity (e.g., a search for the missing object). By contrast, a question differs from a statement. A statement is a declaration of a point of view, opinion, belief, or perceived "truth." Statements tend toward stability and may not be open to change or debate (e.g., "This is a country for white men"). At the same time, the statement conceals ambiguity, and ignores other questions or concerns, such as which white men—rich or poor, smart or dumb, sane or insane? And what about white women and children.

Questions, by contrast, tend toward flux. Like a river in constant movement, questions can bring new perspectives and contribute to the creation of new realities. Questioning is the action of calling forth an issue, asking, pursuing, or seeking. At the same time it is an invitation for others to join in. In chapter 1, we used an imaginary scenario to show how questions can be used to expand the therapist's awareness of context and of what is going on. Context is the arbitrary boundary drawn around a set of relationships, behavior, and emotions within a particular time frame in which verbal and nonverbal communications become meaningful. Questions can be used rhetorically (e.g., "Have you stopped lying to the American people?") and in a wide variety of other ways—for example, to interrogate and expose (e.g., "Where were you last night?!"), accuse, judge, or criticize (e.g., "When will you grow up?!"), clarify (e.g., "What did you mean by that?"), explore (e.g., "How do we get there from here?"), create doubt (e.g., "Are you telling the truth?"), expand awareness (e.g., "What else is missing?"), reflect on the past or anticipate the future (e.g., "How did our ancestors face hardship?"), and make connections between people (e.g., "When father is sad, how do other family members respond?"). Some questions that are raised to make connections (e.g., "How shall we respond to father's sadness?") have been misread as a sign of stupidity or helplessness, and perceived as an invitation to take over. Questions can be used to affirm (e.g., "When did you achieve such brilliance in your work?"), etc. We can see that these questions overlap and may serve multiple purposes. For example, an exploratory question (e.g., "How do you get there from here?") will also serve the purpose of expanding awareness, especially if one had not thought about the topic before. The meanings of questions are context-dependent and presuppose a mutual understanding of the questioner's intention, tone, use of words, demeanor, and the party to whom the question is addressed.

Questions may appear to have fixed meanings. In the courtroom, for example, questions are often used to interrogate. In the classroom questions are often used to test knowledge or for clarification. In therapy questions are often used to elicit information, explore, expand awareness, plant a thought or idea, or suggest a course of action. But questions are not limited to these particular contexts. Questions have been used to interrogate in the context of therapy when a series or a line of questions are asked, or in the classroom (e.g., "Did you do your homework assignment?"). Exploratory questions have been used in the courtroom to elicit new information or create connections in the mind of the jury. The purpose of the questions and the ends they serve vary enormously. We may ask, What purposes or interest do questions serve in the contexts in which they are used? Whose interest are being served or undermined? What questions are raised and what questions are suppressed?

The Use of Questions in Training Programs

I have emphasized the important role questions can play when training family therapists. They can open up new and unexplored areas, evolve a new perspective, maintain the status quo, or stimulate the imagination and spur one to action. They can reveal contradictions or inconsistencies. Questions may also be frightening and thus shut down communication. They may invade privacy, start a rumor, or evoke unpleasant memories that cause a great deal of anxiety or possible heart attack, cancer, or accident. In short, questions can be used in ways that are helpful or in ways that are not helpful, or even harmful.

Consider the following hypothetical case. It will be used to help trainees see the role of questions in family therapy and how questions can expand their awareness of what is going on. Mrs. Johnson and Jane, her 12-year-old daughter, were referred to the family counseling center for therapy by their doctor. Mrs. and Mr. Johnson have been divorced for approximately one year. Mr. Johnson lives in the neighborhood and within a few blocks of his ex-wife and daughter. Jane and her father appeared to have had a good relationship, and it was described by the referring party as "amicable." The other day, Mr. Johnson smashed his way into his ex-wife and daughter's home and attacked Jane. The police were called and his daughter was taken to the hospital. Upon examination, the doctor made a formal report to the Child Protective Agency, which was investigating. Mrs. Johnson and Jane were shocked by this attack and felt that their lives had been permanently changed. They talked with their minister, who also encouraged them to seek counseling to deal with the trauma of this event. Mrs. Johnson would like an appointment as soon as possible for Jane and herself.

In a training session with family therapists, I may select three or four trainees to read and discuss among themselves this information from the referring party. The remaining trainees leave the room so they will not be influenced by the referral information. Once the information about the Johnson family has been shared among the three or four trainees and questions of clarification raised, I will invite the remaining trainees back into the room to listen to the discussion of the case. The three or four trainees who read the Johnson case are invited to sit in an inner circle to discuss it. The remaining trainees form an outer circle.

During the discussion the trainees in the outer circle record the questions that come to mind as a result of observing the inner circle's process and listening to their discussion. After about seven to ten minutes of listening to the discussion, I ask members of the outer circle to reflect on what they have heard, what kinds of questions are being raised or pursued, and what questions are not being raised, i.e., what is missing? For example, what questions are raised or not raised about Mrs. Johnson, Jane, or Mr. Johnson? What questions are raised or not raised about the referring doctors relationship to the family? The trainees in the outer circle have not read the referral information, and therefore have not been influenced by it as have the members of the inner circle. Members of the outer circle can bring curiosity, fresh questions, and a different level of awareness into the discussion. There is an exchange of information. New connections can be made about the Johnson family that will expand the awareness of the trainees. This process of bringing fresh questions and eliciting different points of view is enhanced when the trainees come from different orientations—genders and ethnic and cultural backgrounds—and are encouraged to share and learn from these differences.

There is also an opportunity to identify the purpose and impact of certain questions. Of course, no one knows ahead of time the actual impact a question will have on family members or on the therapist. The actual impact will depend on the family's living context, unique organization and structure, and the interaction between family members and the therapist. Therapists are also influenced by the questions they raise and the responses of the family to them. Trainees learn to distinguish between questions that help to intensify or deintensify a situation, and between methods that are intrusive or less intrusive, and yield relevant information.

Ideally, therapeutic questions are used to orient, envision, ground, elicit information, challenge, and make connections between past, present and an anticipated future. Therefore, the purpose of this exercise is to help students to see the important role questions can play in expanding awareness and in eliciting and organizing information in the context of therapy. Questions are never neutral. They convey beliefs, attitudes, perceptions, and intentions. They convey levels of awareness and communicate certain values and interest. Questions have impact. Through the use of this and similar exercises trainees can reflect on the important role of questions, identify a range of questions, and learn to distinguish between helpful and unhelpful uses of questions in the therapy context. Questions can be based on a deep respect for people, and asked in ways that reveal caring for others.

The Use of Questions in Systemic Family Therapy

Systemic family therapists have called attention to the various uses of questions.[1] Questions have been used in systemic family therapy to stimulate curiosity and to increase awareness of the interplay of past, present, and future in situations where a family member feels trapped by an unacceptable past. They have been used to evoke changes in family patterns, or to track the sequence of behavior around a problem, or to elicit specific information about specific hypotheses.[2] Different kinds of questions—such as lineal, circular, strategic and reflexive—have been identified and distinguished in the literature.[3] These kinds of questions are used in a variety of ways. They may be used to orient therapists to the problematic situation and enable them to become aware of their own biases. They may be used to influence the family or stimulate therapeutic change. The above list of uses of questions in the family therapy literature is not exhaustive. It represents only a small sampling of ways systemic family therapists have used questions.

The focus of these questions is on the immediate context of the therapy and on how better questions can be raised to find out about family patterns, organization, and structure, and about the interaction between therapists and help seekers. In our hypothetical case involving the Johnson family, the therapist would attempt to understand what is going on in the family through an understanding of the problem. The therapist would attempt to understand the problem by eliciting information about differences within the family and changes in beliefs, expectations, behavior, and relationships among family members. The therapist might ask, "Who needs to be involved in the therapy?" "Where is the pain and the hope in this situation?" "Who appeared to be the most (and least) affected by the divorce?" "Have things been better or worse at home for Jane and her mother since the parents divorced?" "When do things appear to be going well between Jane and her father?" "What was the relationship like between Jane and her mother?" "Does the father appear to be better or worse off since the divorce?" "When things are going well between Jane and her mother, how does the father respond?" "What has been lost and gained as a result of the attack on Jane?" "Which new ideas about family relationships best fit the Johnson family since the attack on Jane?" The objective of the questions is to understand what provoked the attack on Jane by understanding the changes in family belief and patterns, and to track the sequence of behavior around the problem. The aim of the therapy is to provide a new context for living that includes safety for family members and empowerment to make the changes they desire, and to offer choice and hope.

The wider cultural context, which will soon be our focus, may or may not be seen as immediately relevant. We note, for example, that there was no mention of the cultural, or ethnic, background of the family in the referral information of our hypothetical case with the Johnson family. There was no information about demographic shifts or the immediate neighborhood or living situation of the family, and no information about societal conditions or historical factors that might be relevant. Questions can also orient us toward the wider social contexts in which the relationship between therapist and help seeker is embedded.

Questions Can Raise New Awareness about Wider Social Contexts

The question with which this chapter began was: "Can a negro, whose ancestors were imported into this country, and sold as slaves, become a member of the political community formed and brought into existence by the Constitution of the United States?" The United States Supreme Court in 1856 answered the question in the negative. It was not the federal government's intention to include African Americans. They were defined by white society as slaves, not citizens. They were rejected and condemned to a permanent noncitizen and inferior status. This decision of utter rejection, painful to African Americans, was handed down by the highest court in the land. It represented the dominant perspective of the white power system. In the words of former president Andrew Johnson, "This is a country for white men." The high court decision of 1856 was designed to forever fix a place of inferiority for black presence in the United States. If African Americans despaired, gave up hope, or turned away from God, it would have been understandable. But they did not. The question meant something very different for them. They would answer in the affirmative and stride toward freedom.

The high court decision represented for African Americans an evil to be overcome by the cooperation of human and divine agency.

The river of their struggle was wide. By "river of struggle" I mean African Americans' efforts to be included as full participants, respected and equal members of the political community. It is African Americans' turbulent journey from bondage toward freedom, self-determination, and full humanity in the Western Hemisphere. Their struggle has been a turbulent journey toward freedom, self-determination, and full humanity from the time of their capture in Africa, the crossing of the great water, in bondage and freedom into the present. The struggle for freedom has been communal in nature. This journey marked by struggle sought to transform the closed society of the South, and the de facto segregated society of the North. That journey has navigated a course marked by progress and setbacks, tragic loss and questionable gains, betrayal, a sense of purpose, hope, resilience and resistance, improvisation or creative response, the emergence of new meanings, and an uncommon faith in divine providence. The river also represents continuity. It connects us with ancestors, a continuous line of descendants and connections that can enrich our understanding of the present. It influences our daily walk and talk in conscious and unconscious ways. The ways this river flows through our lives and the way we navigate its waters today, is open to interpretation and reinterpretation. The fresh questions we bring will help us to navigate. As present-day navigators we can become creators, strategists, and mediators of change and hope, or we can become destructive, nonreflective, and fools hopelessly trapped in the diabolic schemes of others. The choice is not as clear-cut as the words may imply. The river of our struggle is often fraught with ambiguity, dangers, and unforeseen twists and turns.

It was mutual caring, the care of each for the other, amidst struggle that made resistance possible, inspired hope, and provided the resolve to continue the collective struggle. For example, William Still records the story of a fugitive slave, Wesley Harris, who was shot during a failed escape and hospitalized in a tavern until he was well enough to be returned to slavery. While recuperating, he began to make plans for another escape. He sought the help of the cook, a black woman, and two other friends, who bought him the things he needed in order to make his escape from the hospital-tavern successful.

> I asked one of my friends to get me a rope. He got it. I kept it about me four days in my pocket; in the meantime I procured three nails. On Friday night, October 14th, I fastened my nails in under the window sill; tied my rope to the nails, threw my shoes out of the window, put the rope in my mouth, then took hold of it with my well hand, clambered into the window, very weak, but I managed to let myself down to the ground.[4]

He managed to get to a secure hiding place, where he remained for a few hours. Then, "A swift horse was furnished by James Rogers, and a colored man found to conduct me to Gettysburg. Instead of going direct to Gettysburg, we took a different road, in order to shun our pursuers, as the news of my escape had created general excitement."[5] Without the help of many others, resistance to and escape from slavery would not have been possible. The escape of Wesley Harris was aided by the Underground Railroad, an organized effort that assisted many fugitive slaves to make it to freedom. Implicit in this experience is a psychology and strategy of resistance, survival, and self-other affirmation that developed among nineteenth-century African Americans. In their own way, they began to answer the question, "Can a negro, whose ancestors were imported into this country, and sold as slaves, become a member of the political community?"

How does one explain the resistance of African Americans to attempts to exclude, control, and completely demoralize them, such as the 1857 Supreme Court decision? It was their collective belief in divine providence, shared memory, and manner of caring that sustained their hope. This sense of collective memory and practice of mutual care must be part of therapeutic strategies for African Americans today. The 1857 Supreme Court decision meant that African Americans in their personal, family, and communal life had to struggle harder for the day of freedom. They helped one another and suffered together. As a result they became strategists, navigators of hope, and mediators of change. They developed social roles and religious resources more complex than those of the white society that held them in contempt. For example, Cordelia Loney of Fredericksburg, Va., a slave of Mrs. Joseph Cahell, was held in contempt, her children were sold, and she was frequently flogged by the madam even though she was regarded as Mrs. Cahell's "most efficient and reliable maid-servant."[6] During a visit to Philadelphia with her mistress, Cordelia requested counsel from the Vigilance Committee and was successful in gaining her freedom. Mrs. Cahell returned to Fredericksburg alone. After gaining her freedom in Philadelphia, Cordelia Loney learned that her former mistress could not manage her life without her. "Her mistress was seriously puzzled to imagine how she would get her shoes and stockings on and off; how she would get her head combed."[7] A certain doctor of divinity of a local Episcopal church took it upon himself to locate Cordelia Loney in Philadelphia and have her return to Mrs. Cahell. The reverend doctor met a black man whom he believed would reveal Cordelia Loney's whereabouts. The black man was Thomas Dorsey, a successful entrepreneur in Philadelphia and a former fugitive slave. Mr. Dorsey remained an enigma to the Reverend, who quoted Scripture in an attempt to justify black slavery. Mr. Dorsey drew from his own spiritual depths as he made reply to the Reverend, "telling him that Cordelia had as good a right to her liberty as he had, or her mistress . . . that God had never intended one man to be the slave of another."[8] Cordelia Loney had freedom on her mind and fled to Canada. "Being a member of the Baptist Church, and professing to be a Christian," she was persuaded that God would open a way for her in freedom and in the strange new land where she had fled.[9] In this way, Cordelia Loney, Thomas Dorsey, and thousands of others like them developed social roles and religious resources more complex than those of the people who held them in contempt.

Nineteenth-century African Americans had to improvise in the face of danger, develop secret ways to communicate, draw on religious resources, and depend on their faith in God's deliverance in ways unparalleled in the white society of their day. In the process they created alternatives within the society that oppressed them, and transformed themselves from mere victims to agents of hope

63

who worked for change. Why has their experience of pain, resistance, and hope been ignored as a fount of knowledge by mainstream mental health services? Such ignorance and/or devaluing of African American experience has left much of white society (and much of therapeutic training) unable to integrate positive religious or spiritual understandings or evolve relevant cross-cultural and therapeutic knowledge in an increasingly multicultural and religiously pluralistic society.

Why is it important to remember this history of struggle against one of the most virulent forms of institutionalized racism? There are at least three reasons. First, there is a history of ignoring or trivializing the cultural and spiritual resources of African Americans as overly emotional, primitive, and anti-intellectual. This history is reflected in mainstream mental health services and pastoral care. To ignore the struggles and contributions of African American and other ethnic minorities to indigenous mental health results in impoverished views of mental health. Second, mental health services such as therapy and pastoral care are social practices shaped by the dominant culture. Whether intended or not, these practices mediate prevailing views of purity-pollution, or healthy and sick persons, as well as normative views of race, class, and gender. These prevailing views inform criteria for membership in professional associations and for supervision, and they legitimate who qualifies as a practitioner and who does not. When the history of white superiority, colonial rule, slavery, and genocide is denied or forgotten, then it will be impossible to recognize how that history is manifest in present-day practices. Even when history is remembered, still there is oppression forged in the name of "right," "truth," "ownership," etc. But when history is not recognized, it is much harder to name and resist the old forms of oppression that find new channels of expression. Third, in our individualistic culture a naive attitude toward racism is often justified as a matter of personal preference, that is, "I prefer not to associate with blacks, Jews, Asians, Hispanics, or "I like individual blacks, etc." When society is reduced to individuals and families and the historical context is not remembered, then it is easy to rationalize racism and other forms of oppression as a matter of personal preference. It is important, therefore, to remember this history of oppression and struggle against it if we want to help transform it. That history lays bare white assumptions about nonwhites, and it is only by understanding these that white therapists can better understand the part they play and work with others toward transforming the mainstream. "Even well-intended [whites] still live in a state of denial regarding just how deep seated white supremacy is in the culture. So what happens is race is understood primarily in personal terms."[10]

Therapists, trained in an individualistic culture and in the conventions of individualistic psychology, may find it difficult to know what to do with sociological or historical information like that given above. But family therapists claim a systems orientation; therefore, they ought to be interested in the ways history influences social patterns and the details of everyday life. Once I gave an address at a convention of pastoral caregivers. After the address, a pastoral care practitioner approached and told me that he did not see how the sociological and historical information I gave could be of help to him because he does not deal with the population of people (black and/or mixed race) to which I was referring. In addition, he did not think there was anything he could do about societal problems in individual therapy, or psychotherapy. There the primary focus is on the inner life of the individual. Unwittingly, he made an important point. When the private inner life of the lone individual is the primary focus, then it is difficult to see the operation of systemic influences. Consequently, it is difficult to grasp different social and cultural levels of meaning and how they are woven together in prevailing understandings of the self. It is hard to see how the self is constituted and renewed by its many relations over time. We may not see how the past interacts with and helps to shape our life and practice in the present when the private life of the individual is the primary focus of attention. What he missed was the fact that therapy itself is a historically and socially constituted practice. The past interacts with the present in subtle ways, and systemic forms of oppression and resistance are transmitted through family relations and through contexts of therapy. Forms of oppression are internalized and reproduced through social practices that mediate societal norms and reflect the prevailing ideologies of society.[11]

Perhaps few would raise the question of black presence in the United States in the same tone that it was raised in 1857. But what knowledgeable citizen would deny that white control of institutions and values supporting white supremacy and other Eurocentric interests continues to determine the direction of the American mainstream? Therefore, we are saddened but not surprised when a present-day candidate for the presidency of the United States can comfortably say: "When we say we will put America first, we mean also that our Judaeo-Christian values are going to be preserved and our Western heritage is going to be handed down to future generations and not dumped into some landfill called multiculturalism."[12] What is the alternative to a multiracial and multicultural society in the United States? In this regard, George Furniss's work is of paramount importance to caregivers. In *The Social Context of Pastoral Care,* he argued that pastoral caregivers must make the everyday social life of people and their definitions of situations the object of investigation.[13] Their definitions of situations arise from their social position, which has been influenced by history. In those definitions are to be found resources for spiritual renewal, mental health, and social transformation. But when such definitions are ignored, then it will be difficult to recognize how the past is reproduced in the present. And it will be difficult for therapists to acknowledge the part they play in cultural reproduction or the kinds of questions they could raise to help bring new levels of awareness.

Consider the following episode. It happened recently. I waited at the Family Counseling Center for a 4:00 P.M. therapy appointment with a black family. By 4:30 P.M. they had not shown. A black social worker requested the appointment with the counseling center, and a white therapist (psychologist) made the appointment by sending a letter to the family.

The family of three (mother, father, and son) were originally referred to the Family Service Agency four years earlier because the 11-year-old son was bullying, fighting, and stealing at school. Information about an extended family, social network, neighborhood, religious affiliation, civic or political participation was not gathered. The mother and father were divorced. The son, age 11, was living with his mother when the family first made contact with the family counseling agency. Now, four years later and at age 15, the son was living with his father. This black family had also sought help from other white counseling agencies. The last therapist to see the family reported that the mother (the family member most frequent in attendance) had gotten something from the therapy. The therapist was not specific.

I had not yet met the family. I was looking forward to meeting them for the first time at the 4:00 P.M. appointment. When 4:30 arrived, I surmised that they probably were not going to come. I wondered why. Several questions came to mind. Did they not get the letter? Had they called but not gotten through? Did the divorced parents not want to attend the same meeting? Were they unable to make the time due to work conflict or transportation difficulties? Was someone ill? Were there other reasons?

My white colleague decided to make a phone call to see if the mother had received the letter. The mother had received it and said that she did not think she was going to be able to make it. My colleague pressed for clarity. Was it because of time conflict or difficulty in getting to the counseling center? The mother then said, "Been there, done that and it doesn't help!" She had been to most all of the white family counseling agencies and had "gotten nothing out of the meetings." She then said that she definitely would not come back unless her son was willing to talk. She saw no value in coming for herself. The conversation appeared to be coming to an end. The mother was not offering new information, rather, she repeated her resolve to not come again. She "had gotten nothing out of it."

My colleague then asked if I would talk to the mother. I was reluctant because it was clear to me that the mother had not found this approach, that is to say, therapy in a white setting, useful. My colleague handed me the phone by saying to the mother, "I would like for my colleague to talk with you." I introduced myself to the mother and told her that I understood that she was not interested in coming; that I was looking forward to meeting her and her son's father to see if it was possible to be of help with their son. But it was clear to me from what she had said that coming to the Center had not been a helpful experience. The mother's tone appeared to have changed. New information was offered. She said that possibly her ex-husband had forgotten the appointment. She offered to talk with him and see if he was interested in coming. Again, she made it clear that she was not interested in coming for herself, but if it would help her son, then she would come for his sake. She then asked about the times when we were available. These questions and her offer to contact her ex-husband appeared to signal an openness that was not there before I talked with her.

After the phone call, my colleague and I reviewed what had just happened. I wondered what it was that was not helpful to this family. My colleague observed that the mother's tone seemed to have softened when I came on the phone. She wondered if we should try again to engage the family in therapy. The father had not attended therapy meetings in the past, although he was invited. The mother came with their son. After a few meetings, the son refused to attend, and soon the mother stopped coming. My colleague reflected that the mother felt responsible and blamed herself for her son's behavior and that the sense of blame was reinforced when she came to therapy. This view was confirmed in a follow-up meeting with the black social worker. Not only did the mother feel blamed in the therapy sessions, she was blamed by the neighbors, who believed that her son had stolen from them. How would this family's experience be different if we were able to reengage them in therapy? What could we offer that would make a difference? It is easier to see the pain than it is to see the hope in this situation. Hope lies in the possibility that family members may see themselves as resourceful and contributing to the resolution of their difficulty and toward the growth of each other, whether they live together or separate. Would the experience of therapy be helpful if all three family members were involved, the limitations of therapy acknowledged, and their cultural resources made central to therapy?

Looking back, would the experience of giving and receiving help have been different had the therapists been black or if the therapeutic team been of mixed race? I suggested to my colleague that initial involvement of the whole family was important; that race, culture, and gender roles were probably unacknowledged factors. Had the therapists been knowledgeable about and able to tap the cultural and spiritual resources of this black family, would their experience with therapy have been different and helpful? I do not know why the mother changed her mind. But I know that there was a shift in her attitude about coming to the Center. Perhaps she felt encouraged by the possibility of working with an African American therapist. If the family's past experiences with white institutions had been acknowledged, and their resources and structures for coping addressed, they might have experienced greater support.

It is not possible to say specifically how the family's experience and the experiences of the therapists have been shaped by the past. There are many levels of meaning that could be assessed, including: (a) transgenerational influences from the parent's family of origin; (b) influences of the past that are reflected in the practice of therapy and that support prevailing ideologies of race, power, and gender relations; (c) how the background, experience, and attitude of the white therapists influenced therapy; (d) the family's past experiences with white and black institutions; and (e) cultural resources available to them now. If the history of racism and cultural oppression is not understood as a conditioning influence at all of these levels, then it will be impossible to understand how the immediate context of therapy functions to mediate established inferior/superior relationship patterns. "Racism is often invisible to those who do not experience its effects directly and services can prove inaccessible or insensitive to those whose history includes slavery or colonialism or whose heritage and life experience differs from the mainstream."[14]

Historical experiences cited in this chapter have, with a few exceptions, seldom been drawn on to positively inform, supplement, or offer correction to the major schools of psychiatry and psychology. Psychiatry and psychology, with their main roots in nineteenth-century Europe, represent ethnocentric bodies of knowledge. Psychological theories have indeed portrayed the slave's religion as primitive and a source of psychopathology or escapism. In this way, these theories have functioned as vehicles of racism.[15]

For African Americans, their religion was historically their primary mental health resource. It formed the basis of their self-help networks and therapeutic expressions. It was a resource to generate images of their worth and competence, which differed from the negative judgments of the society that surrounded them. It was the

69

backbone of their struggle to survive. It was the central motivating force inspiring their freedom struggle. It informed their vision of a new kind of society, a beloved community. As a result, they were able to carry the pain *and* the hope.

The theme of this book is that historical memory, the legacy of the slave's religion, and the present-day struggles of African Americans form a continuous stream of spiritual experiences and are resources to be tapped and augmented. They can inform research and help to balance or correct the theory, concepts, and metaphors that inform therapeutic practice. In African American experience, past and present, is to be found religious beliefs and spiritual resources that are vital to successful therapy and spiritual growth. This statement takes on significance when viewed in the context of the virulent history of racism. That history assumes the innate superiority of white Americans and the inherent inferiority of African Americans and other nonwhites. The fact that African Americans are overrepresented in prison, welfare, and unemployment roles is often used to justify the continuation of practices steeped in racist ideologies.

Family therapy can be an opportunity for reflexivity, that is, it can be an opportunity to become aware of the destructive and creative influences that operate within the mainstream of society, therapy, and the river of our experience. Ideally, therapy increases a sense of agency within the family as family members review the past and navigate the present. It can serve proleptical functions, that is, enable family members to envision and forge a different future. Family members can do this by drawing on the spiritual and cultural resources that are potentially available to them. In short, family therapy can be a resource to help family members become a transforming influence upon self and community. On the other hand, it can be used to divert help and reinforce demoralizing patterns of the past (under the guise of helping) and thereby serve to maintain the status quo of inferior/superior power relations.

Questions Can Link the Context of Therapy with Society

In light of the case just presented and generalizing from it, I identify four categories and list questions under each as examples of the kind of questions that can be used during the initial phases of therapy or throughout the course of therapy with African American families. The following questions are similar to those that appeared in chapter 1, but they also differ in that each new situation or context will stimulate different issues and concerns and therefore different questions. The levels of reflexive questions below are suggested with the understanding that it is desirable to have present as many family members as possible who are related to the presenting dilemma. Each family member's definition of situations and voice is crucial to the resolution or maintenance of the difficulty at hand. Such a meeting may take place in the family's home or some other place of mutual agreement. The questions are intended to increase the reflexive capacity of family members by linking awareness of the past with the present. They are intended to enhance a sense of moral agency among family members by enabling persons to experience themselves as resourceful in response to one another. These questions are intended to help tap spiritual resources such as expressions of compassion and understanding, to evoke new awareness and change in attitude, and to restore purpose and meaning in life, along with trust and joy. Questions sometimes generate further questions and an expanded awareness of what is possible in life. In this regard, reflexive questions move up and down between levels as well as back and forth. Reflexive questions also move back and forth between the therapist's and the client's perceptions of what is going on. They move between awareness of cultural context and context of therapy and between prevailing and marginalized ideologies. Questions can help family members relate to spiritual values and ritual practices in the hope of transforming their situation and themselves.

Reflexive Questions

The function of reflexive questions is to increase awareness about what is going on between therapist, family members, and their environment—to identify cultural and spiritual resources and make better decisions. The first category contains the presession questions. They are questions that therapists can raise and think about before the meeting with the family begins. The following are among the questions that can be raised:

Level 1: Presession Questions. These are questions to stimulate awareness about the therapists use of self.

What understandings does the therapist bring to the first meeting with the family, and what informs this understanding?

What is the therapist's awareness of her or his own culture, gender, ethnic background, and spiritual orientation in relation to reports about the family? How can these awarenesses become resourceful?

How is the therapist being influenced by information about the family, their work, play, and living environment?

How flexible and creative is the therapist willing or able to be under the circumstances?

What is the therapist's awareness of her or his own limitations, and how can awareness of limitations become a resource rather than a liability?

How does the therapist explain what is going on (i.e., what language, images, artistic expressions, metaphors, myths or stories, proverbs or sacred texts come to mind or may be employed, and for what purposes)?

What is the therapist's knowledge about the family's culture, ethnic background, spiritual orientation?

What worries the therapist the most (or least) about the family's dilemma?

What kinds of questions has the therapist not yet asked or needs to learn to ask about the family's own experiences?

How can the therapist show respect to the family?

What might the therapist do with the family's offerings (i.e., comments, questions, suggestions, insights, humor, metaphors, sighs, looks or demeanor, silences, surprises, etc)?

Level 2: Context of Therapy. Questions about the context of therapy include the following:

How is the family organized?

How familiar is the therapist with the family's neighborhood?

How safe or at risk is the family or a family member in their living environment?

What are the therapist's working assumptions about the aims of therapy and how individuals and/or families can be helped?

What are the pressures on the therapist to succeed?

How congruent or different is the context of therapy from the everyday world of the family or family members seeking help?

What are some current cultural myths or stereotypes about gender, religious orientation, ethnicity, or the racial background of the family?

What are some cultural strengths?

What research is available concerning the family's presenting problem?

Is the meeting place or therapy room inviting?

Can a context for therapeutic help be created?

What are the limitations of therapy?

Level 3: The Therapy Session. These questions might be used during the session to guide therapist and family.

What is the referring issue (or what is the problem/question) and how does the family view it?

Who initiated the referral and how is the referring party related to the family or to the presenting problem?

What social, economic, political, health, educational issues or institutions impinge upon the family's presenting issue?

Who is most worried (and who least worried) about the problem/question?

What do they want to achieve in therapy, and what is their idea of help?

Does the family have a religious affiliation or background?

How are decisions made in the family?

Who are the important role models in the family?

Who are the important role models outside the family?

Are there special sayings, proverbs, metaphors, or images family members use to describe their experience?

How does the family cope under stress?

What patterns or relationship configurations maintain the presenting problem or family pain?

What strategies do they use when things go wrong?

What values are most important to them?

How does the family communicate with itself (with insiders) and with others (outsiders)?

How is the family seen by outsiders?

How do family members express strong emotions?

Is there evidence of physical, emotional, or spiritual violence in the family?

Have there been recent changes in the family?

How do family members explain what is going on, and how do they believe they can best be helped?

What cultural, spiritual, or religious resources are available to the family, and how have those resources been employed?

What is the therapist's initial hypothesis about why the family is coming or being referred at this time?

What does the hypothesis include or exclude?

What has already been done (what attempts) to resolve the issue?

Level 4: Post-Therapy Session. These questions might be reflected upon after the family meeting and in preparation for a follow-up meeting. They are questions about resources in the immediate environment and questions about the internal resources of the immediate family.

What new information and questions emerged?

What emotions were expressed or not expressed?

Was there evidence of violence within the family?

Was there evidence of violence to the family from the society?

What meanings did family members assign to the problem at hand?

What meaning does the family assign to its environment (i.e., fate, good luck, bad luck, human evil, divine providence)?

Where does the family live, and what dangers and resources exist in the family's immediate environment (e.g., natural, spiritual, physical, and social dangers and resources)?

How did family members express their sense of justice or fair play?

What has been the family's experience with key social institutions such as housing, labor, and transportation, political, health, education, legal, religious, economic, etc.

What stories did family members tell about coping under stress?

In what support network and/or kinship systems does the family participate?

Who should attend future meetings?

What encourages or inspires this family and gives them a sense of direction when things go wrong?

What is their image(s) of themselves—i.e., how do they describe themselves at various times (what language, symbols, metaphors do they employ)?

Where are their strengths and how do they use them?

How do family members express (or manifest) their value system, beliefs, and convictions—their worldview?

What rituals does the family engage in and to what end?

How are money, rewards, and punishments used?

The responses to the above questions will stimulate movement up and down, back and forth between and within different levels of meaning. The relationship between the levels is circular and reflexive.16 Since every family and family member brings their own unique way of seeing the world and communicating, the therapist must stay alert to what is going on between self, family members, the presenting problem, and the context of therapy. Therefore, the questions are not meant to be used insensitively, nor asked as if one were being interrogated, nor asked for the sake of asking questions. When a questions is not helpful or is not meaningfully engaging the therapist and family members around the presenting problem, then it is time to do something different. Therefore, the questions are in-tended to open and guide exploration, to make connections, and to deepen awareness of the family's use of resources, the therapist's use of self, and the emerging context of therapy. The goal is to give the family reason to hope by working with them to increase their reflective capacities and their sense of moral agency, and to bring their spiritual resources into play. The questions are designed to open doors and allow the therapist and the family to develop awareness in a context that facilitates mutual care, is therapeutic and educative, and empowers the family to make desired changes. The idea of mutual care is important in traditions of African American care. It is as important to give care as it is to receive it. The mutual care is an extension of the self and a sign of gratitude. Gratitude is an expression of health. Hence the questions "How does the therapist show respect?" and "What will the therapist do with the family's offerings?" are important.

Implications for Therapy

We return to the case above. When black family members first come to therapy, they are actively testing and evaluating the interpersonal environment between the therapist and themselves. They notice the ambience of the setting as well as how their offerings—in the form of questions, comments, facial expressions, or other gestures—are being received. This is to say, the emotional climate of therapy is of primary importance to African Americans. Issues of acceptance or rejection, respect and self-esteem, sense of compassion, and per-ceived understanding are of primary concern. Even if family mem-bers give the appearance of being uninvolved or unresponsive, they are, nevertheless, actively monitoring the verbal and nonverbal ex-changes in the therapy setting. It becomes the basis for deciding whether or not they will continue or terminate the relationship. For example, after I moved to a new city, a former black counselee wrote and asked for a referral. I recommended a very good thera-pist who was also white. After their first meeting, the black counse-lee wrote again and said, "She is a good therapist and told me most of the things you have told me (except you have more compassion and understanding)." Psychologist Adelbert H. Jenkins observed, "What we may . . . see in the early stages of therapy with Afro-

American clients is an active use of the everyday human capacities for affective assessment that Blacks tend to rely on more in this society."[17] When blacks do not continue in therapy, it is sometimes interpreted as lack of motivation, or as evidence that they are not able to benefit from therapy, or some other reason that attributes the discontinuance to the help seeker. Whether it is recognized or not, the white therapist is a symbol of a society that treats black people as inferior. Therefore, the therapist's competence will be measured by the warmth, accessibility, respect, and personal interest she or he communicates to the black counselee. This is not surprising when one considers that a part of the survival strategies of African Americans is that they have been keen observers and interpreters of their environment. Their lives have depended on being keen observers. Therefore, the white therapist will need to establish a warm, accepting, and genuine relationship with each family member in the first two or three sessions. When they do continue, the continuance may be attributed to a well-motivated counselee and a good fit between therapist and client values. In both instances, therapy as a cultural practice that mediates prevailing ideologies of superior/inferior race and social power relations may be missed.

When the mother said, "Been there, done that and it does not help," she was giving her own short-hand assessment of her participation in therapy. Given the circumstances that brought her to the therapist's office—i.e., a son who causes trouble at school—it is important to understand what coming to the therapist's office means to her and other family members. If it is the case that coming to a therapist induces a sense of cultural awkwardness for many black clients, then what are the emotional implications of this situation? What does coming to a white agency for help mean for the family member's sense of self-esteem and competence as parents? What are the consequences for their son's development? If the mother's goal for coming to therapy in the first place was to get help for her son and protect him from additional stress and emotional hurt in a white society, then her efforts (sense of agency) as a single black parent need to be positively acknowledged. Her presence is part of her striving to be a caring and competent parent. Psychologist Adelbert H. Jenkins noted that such expressions of self-agency are seldom noticed by white society. When a black family presents with a serious difficulty it is easier to focus on their perceived tangle of pathology or assume incompetence, and miss the active and purposeful role they play in effecting the course of therapy. "But when black individuals find that they must seek psychological help, they not only bring the maladaptive aspects of their functioning, but they also bring some of the same processes that produce striving for competence and which push them to search for a way out of their dilemmas."[18] Such striving for self-definition is consistent with the black struggle to be free. For these reasons it is vitally important for the therapist to identify family strengths in the past and present, and draw upon them.

I assume that no therapist comes to a first meeting free of values. No one comes to a socially charged encounter such as this one without concerns or without positive or negative prejudices. Therefore, in order to prepare for this first meeting with a black family, the white therapist would need to raise some self-discerning questions, such as, What understandings do I bring to my first meeting with this family and what informs this understanding? Recall that the referral source was the school where a black youngster was reported to be bullying, fighting, and stealing. This report of the youngster already matches a dominant cultural stereotype of black males as savage, aggressive, unruly, and untrustworthy (e.g., stealing). Therefore, the therapist might ask, "What does this report from the school mean to family members, and what do I (the therapist) know (or need to learn) about the social world, neighborhood, or living environment of the family?" This official information (the school's report) about the son's conduct affects relationships within the family and between the family and the school. The son, who was once seen as just a student, is now seen as a troublesome student with whom the authorities must deal.

I assume that the young person's behavior serves a purpose or function in his family as well as in the community. It may be his attempt to solve a perceived problem. What is this young person trying to communicate through his behavior and what is the message from the people and institutions responding? The therapist might ask, "What are family members' explanations for what is going on? How do they see it?" In addition, "What is the background and strengths of the family I am about to see?" "What is my own attitude or predisposition toward such information (bullying, fighting, stealing)?" "Where do I need assistance and how can I best help?" "What in my own background and experience prepares (or hinders) my work with this family?" "What are my beliefs and prejudices (positive or negative) toward black single mothers, or black fathers who have left the house, and their children who get into trouble?" "What role models and other resources give strength or inspiration when things go wrong?" "What further questions do I need to raise in order to be of help?"

These are some self-reflexive questions the therapist might address to self and to the social system (i.e., the school, courts, social services) before meeting with the family for the first time. Some of these questions are appropriate to ask in the session with the family—for example, "Who is most worried about what is happening at school?" "What is likely to happen should the behavior continue?" If the therapist knows very little about the neighborhood or living environment of the family, then he or she will need to find out so that the therapist can have an expanded context for interpreting what is going on. These questions may help to alert the therapist to what she or he is bringing to this first meeting with the family and how the therapist might address some of her or his own issues ahead of time.

If the therapist is of the same ethnic background as the family, she or he will need to ask equally discerning questions, such as what are my own attitudes toward black males that bully, get into fights, and steal. How much of my own experience is being replayed in this event? What are my own beliefs about how to best help this family? How much will their experience with white institutions mirror my own, and how do I not confuse my experience with theirs? How can I help to empower this family to deal with the set of problems they are bringing?

Therapy is a highly institutionalized cultural practice and a conveyor of the dominant culture's values. Sometimes those values are projected onto the black therapist who works with black families. If the black therapist works within a traditional therapeutic framework, then she or he will also be tested and evaluated in terms of values, compassion, understanding, and accessibility. For these reasons, black therapists must also be willing to address feelings about their own blackness being tested as well as address their own attitudes toward black families very different from their own.

Consultation with the Family

The meeting with this family never took place, but I have some further ideas about what would have been useful had we been able to consult with the family. I base these ideas on the information derived from the phone conversation, file notes from previous therapy sessions, and contact with the referring party. Their 15-year-old son was incarcerated and would soon be remanded to his parents. His release date was coming soon. I would act on the black social worker's request for a meeting by calling one or both of the parents to confirm the request and to negotiate an appointment time. Both parents worked and may not have been able to fit the 9-to-5 schedule of many agencies. The phone call would be followed by a letter of confirmation. The appointment would not be for therapy. I would acknowledge that therapy as offered has not been helpful to them. The appointment would be offered as a one-time consultation with the social worker and both parents to address concerns around their son's impending release to their custody, and to work out strategies for managing his return.

The presence of the social worker, with whom the family has worked and whom they trust, would be critical to the success of this consultation. Her presence would be important for her ongoing work with this family. It would also give her additional information about resources at the family service agency and how to use them. Because of her knowledge of the family, their patterns of interaction and surrounding environment, the social worker could fill in certain gaps in the therapist's knowledge. I would want to know how she views the family's strengths and vulnerabilities. What information does she have about extended-family and religious or spiritual resources? In addition, the therapist could visit the neighborhood and gain some firsthand impressions. This would be especially important if other families are referred from this neighborhood.

I would suggest the possibility that both parents from time to time may have felt some blame for their son's behavior; and that perhaps their son too may feel some disappointment for having failed his parents' best expectations, even though he may not express this directly. I would return to the designated goal of the consultation, which is to talk through and work out parental strategies for managing the return of their 15-year-old son from custody. It would be vitally important to identify and build upon family members' existing strengths and seek to augment them. I would have specific questions in mind, such as, "How does the family (mother and father) view the return of their son?" "What questions and/or concerns do they bring?" "What resources can be identified or created for addressing their concerns?" In addition to these questions, what are their expectations of one another, the social worker, and of this consultation? How do they prefer to cooperate or communicate with one another when special needs arise? How can they be mutually supportive? What resources do or can they call on to guide and sustain them during times of parental stress and frustration? How can the consultants best facilitate this consultation and help meet the family's needs? This is the general direction I would recommend for a one-time consultation. I would work with a female colleague in addition to the social worker, whose trust has already been established.

We do not know if extended-family members are available as resources or what networks are available to this family. What we do know is that this black family is challenged with the task of helping its youngest member to grow and develop in a white-dominated society. Already he is falling behind academically and is in trouble with the law at an early age. So the question with which we began comes around: Can this young person, and thousands of others like him, whose ancestors were sold as slaves become free and resourceful members of the political community? Should he survive to adulthood, as did his father, he will influence other lives and perhaps become a parent himself. The kind of member he will become will be answered in part by the response of social institutions, his developing relations to his parents, and his own decision-making activities in the river of struggle that is a part of his heritage. Because he is a vital influence in the stream of life, it is important that he have contact with his wider heritage.

~

5

Time present and time past
Are both perhaps present in time future,
And time future contained in time past.

T. S. Eliot, "Burnt Norton"

There is a world within where for us the great issues
of our lives are determined.

Howard Thurman, *The Creative Encounter*

Develop Depth of Meaning

What are the spiritual strivings that are common in African American communities and families? How can pastoral caregivers tap spiritual resources and help to develop depth of meaning in life—to enrich a tradition, an idea, belief or experience over time through participation and in ways that enable people to mature and fulfill their lives, contribute to the growth of others, make new connections, and integrate past and present experiences? In this chapter, I will focus on how a spiritually oriented lay person tapped spiritual resources.

An Experience of Suffering

I present a case below and show how these ideas about depth of meaning, reflexivity, and sense of agency are worked out in a relationship between a nurse assistant and a patient.[1] The following case provides the context for identifying how a nurse assistant, a lay person, became the primary pastoral caregiver in a time of extreme need. Hence, I will not focus on my role as a trained therapist or pastoral counselor. Instead, I become a scribe and storyteller who attempts to chart the relationship between two black women who would become friends for life. What this says about my own values as a therapist is that I try to build on the strengths that people disclose without minimizing the tragic side of their experience, and frame beneficial lessons from the stories they tell. Telling the story again and identifying its lessons is what this chapter attempts. In this way, I am able to identify the movement of the river that carries important lessons about tapping spiritual resources by developing depth of meaning, reflexivity, and a sense of agency over time.

A black woman in her late thirties called and asked if I would see her concerning some problems she was having in her second marriage. She will be referred to as Martha. Martha had first turned to her pastor for help, as she had done on many other occasions. But she now wanted to work with issues of a long-standing nature, and she would eventually involve the entire family. During the course of our early interviews, she related her story. As a young woman she was deserted by her first husband. This event evoked earlier memories of having been left by her father when death claimed his life at an early age. She was an only child and had been very close to her father. The father had come to rely on her as if she were his helpmate. The father trusted his daughter to handle the family finances more than the mother, and the daughter became a financial expert. Her mother grew envious of her and they were in constant conflict as she proved to be a very able manager and investor of the family's monies. Martha was deeply shaken by her father's untimely death. She not only lost a father, but her best friend as well, and she lost the buffer between her mother and herself. She now felt extremely isolated within her own family and was the object of her mother's continuing hostility. Marriage for her appeared to be a respectable way to leave home.

At the time of her father's death, she was deeply hurt and outraged with God. When her pastor came to visit just prior to the funeral, she cursed the pastor and God in no uncertain terms. As she stated in therapy, "I said some very cruel things to my pastor and about God. Very cruel!"

Martha's first husband deserted her after five hard years of marriage, leaving her to raise their four children alone on limited income. She spoke of her painful and humiliating experiences in the courtroom whenever she pressed for child support. "The white judge had no comprehension of my situation, implied that I was demanding and insinuated that I deserved to be left." In the courts Martha was portrayed as a vindictive woman and inadequate mother. Understandably, these humiliating experiences led her to the place of never again wanting to be financially dependent on a man.

Soon she learned that she had untreatable cancer. That discovery was like the last straw. She became severely depressed. She signed herself into a hospital and determined that she would die. She refused food and went from 140 pounds to 97 pounds. Her life had become unbearable and she came to believe that no one really cared about her, not even God, whom she had already cursed. And there she lay in a hospital bed dying, without the will to live. She had given up.

A nurse assistant who worked the evening shift (typically 3:00 to 11:00 P.M.) noticed this woman who had given up. Late in the evening after work, when the hospital became quiet, the room lights were turned off, and most patients were asleep, this nurse assistant would quietly slip into Martha's room, sit at her bedside, talk to her, read a few familiar passages of Scripture, pray, and quietly hum a spiritual. Martha was unresponsive at first. As the nurse assistant continued her visits, night after night, Martha slowly regained her desire to live. She felt cared for and talked with the nurse assistant. Martha expressed gratitude.

Eventually, this young single mother left the hospital with a new determination to face the challenges of living. Her cancer was rediagnosed and found to be treatable. Today Martha faithfully serves as a deacon in her church and is a successful dean in a university with major responsibility for the budget. The church of her choice has a strong commitment to spiritual renewal and social uplift. There, Martha is active with others who provide educational, economic, moral, and political leadership in the community. In this way she is a part of a freedom movement. She gives back to the community resources that empower people and enable them to move forward.

She had now turned to a pastoral family therapist for help with her second marriage. Her husband, a black man, was a very successful but very private architect. By "very private" I mean he shared very little of himself with the rest of the family, whom he saw as "her family." I will call him John. Martha and John fought constantly. They often went for long periods without speaking directly to each other, and often sent messages to each other through the children. They kept separate bank accounts and he was often short of money and needed to borrow from her. She found this irritating and he resented having to ask for money. Although they both made a lot of money, there never seemed to be enough. Money became a major catalyst for their conflict.

Martha felt that this second marriage, like her first marriage, was not a true marriage because it lacked the warmth, sense of partnership, and nurture she had always wanted to find in marriage and family. She was now made a grandmother by her oldest child, a son, whom she had had difficulty raising. He now lived with his family in a distant city and had infrequent contact with his mother.

Martha's oldest daughter was in college and doing very well. Of her two remaining children, one was nearing the end of high school and soon would enter college. This daughter was also a difficult child to raise and the mother found her overly dependent, outwardly rebellious, and lacking in gratitude. Martha found it difficult to please this daughter and often felt taken advantage of by her. In her turn, this daughter felt that her mother made too many demands on her.

The last child was just entering high school and was considered a very bright and sweet child who had the best relationship of anyone with her stepfather, John. "She is the one who really understands him," said the mother. Her children had been the only real family she had known and soon they would all be gone. It was with the question of having sacrificed, facing loss, lack of nurture, support, and fulfillment in life and marriage that she was now seeking help. Should she let her last child leave home? And will the last child feel free to leave home? If the last child does leave home what will become of her mom and stepfather?

She Drew from Her Depths and Countered Despair

Martha's life had become unbearable and was almost destroyed by the crosscurrents, the swirling personal and social forces that wore her down. But through a caring relationship with a nurse assistant and the capacity for reflexivity, the meaning of her life was deepened and a sense of agency was renewed.

Martha had always seen herself as a religious person. She believed that God is the Supreme Being, is just, and moved purposefully in her life. This faith would be tested by lived experience. Her faith in God, nurtured in the black church, was deeply shaken by the sudden and untimely death of her father.

She cursed God in her despair. As a black woman, she faced defeat through marital failure, and experienced humiliation and shame in the courts. Then she was faced with the shocking news of "terminal cancer." She gave up. But something deep within her remained. The God of her faith did not abandon or leave her without a witness when all hope was gone. Through the nurse assistant Martha's life was empowered in a way that eventually led toward effective action in the wider sociopolitical context of her church life. Her struggle was with an ongoing sense of God's presence in the context of her illness and experience of oppression. The sense of God's presence was mediated through the concrete acts of a hospital nurse assistant. Her response to the nurse assistant can be recognized as the deep movement of her faith answering the call to live. The nurse assistant, moved by the currents of her own faith and care, was able to reach in, reach out, uplift, and stimulate the spiritual resources in healing, which complements medical science.

In light of the case presented above, we can see how certain events and family dynamics, coupled with the effects of racism and sexism, took shape in the family life of Martha. But these currents, while strong, were not the deepest ones moving her life. In therapy, and on the riverbank of this experience, Martha could reflect on the past as strength was renewed. She could review the past in the light of the present as an experience of redemption from indignity and self-hatred and the curse of ongoing sorrow.[2]

In systemic perspective and through active church involvement, Martha's struggle for inner fulfillment is a part of the wider struggle for freedom from oppression. As a sister sufferer and participant in the lives of others, Martha now helps to empower others even as she has been empowered by the people of God.

The metaphor of the river enables us to interpret the case in terms of riverbank (a place for reflection and remembrance), ongoing movement, a surface, undercurrents, and depth dimensions. We are the river. The river is flowing, and yet it is always in the process of becoming even as it moves toward its destination, the sea. To paraphrase Bernard Loomer, "[the river] builds on its past and points to its future. But only the present, which contains the past and envisages the future, is holy ground."[3] By "holy ground" Loomer means that the present is the locus of the really real, where emerging individuals contribute to their own creation out of the confluence of past developments and future anticipations. The present is always in some sense novel and never completely determined by the past out of which it arose. The present is where we can intervene and make a difference. The nurse assistant, for example, was steadily moved by a sense of inner urgency. She recognized that time present was the opportune time to respond to Martha.

Howard Thurman believed that "there is a world within where for us the great issues of our lives are determined." He believed meaning is inherent in life. It arises in the moment as we reflect, reconstruct, and interpret what is going on. Life is purposeful and moves toward the fulfillment of goals. One's sense of purpose can fall short of fulfillment when the alternatives sought are frustrated. Forms of protest will emerge. Martha sought fulfillment as a responsible daughter, a good parent, and as a partner in a happy marriage. When these purposes fell short of fulfillment, she did not give up. She took action to address them by fighting in the courts, by giving her family and children a good enough start in life. When she was down and out, she rallied to the caring acts of a nurse assistant, got out of bed, and reclaimed her life.

Again, she sought to help establish a happy marriage, but had difficulty achieving this. Martha described an event that was, for her, symbolic of the marital relationship and the reason why it was difficult to achieve marital happiness. She said that her husband, John, liked to have the window shades drawn. He would frequently peep out to see who, if anyone, was coming to the house. Martha saw John as hiding and withholding himself. He wanted to know where others stood, but was not willing to reveal, share, or commit himself. John admitted that he found commitment to and trust of others very difficult. He grew up poor and hungry in a rural area of the Deep South and conserved whatever he got. With the exception of a maternal grandmother, he did not feel close to or safe with other family members. He worked to put himself through college and was bright enough to get scholarship assistance through graduate school. Both Martha and John described John as a loner. Martha said that he does not have friends. Whatever friendships they had as a couple were made through Martha's efforts. Entertaining friends in their home frequently became a source of conflict because John would take the position that they could not afford to entertain friends. Socializing was not something John enjoyed. Entertaining became such a bone of contention between them that Martha stopped having friends over.

When Martha first called for an appointment to talk about her unhappiness in the marriage, I asked her to come with her husband. She said he would never come to counseling. Martha's reason for seeking me out in the first place was that I had the credentials that her husband would find hard to disrespect. But she believed that he would never come to therapy because he could never entrust himself to such a process. She said this with a sense of conviction. She stated her husband's understanding of therapy when she said that it was too intimate a relationship for him and one should never tell a stranger one's personal business.

There is some reality to this. Many African Americans share the belief that therapy is for white folks, and it is not something that black folks do. Therapy means baring your soul to a stranger, and that means putting your business in the street. They had been to therapy once before and with someone familiar to them. Their trust was betrayed and this confirmed John's belief that you should not reveal your personal affairs to anyone. I asked her to please try and convince him to come. She did, and to her amazement, John came. He continued to come and eventually requested some sessions on his own. Money was always a problem for John. He did not like the idea of having to pay for something so intangible as talk therapy. Giving and sharing of himself was not something to which he was accustomed.

Martha, on the other hand, preferred to have the window shades open. She believed that it was important to conserve, but she also wanted intimacy in a trusting relationship. Trust and intimacy were for her hallmarks of a true marriage and happiness. She was unhappy in the marriage because she believed that John had misrepresented himself as an open and sharing person during their courtship. Then he gave all the appearances of being intimate and generous. She said that after they were married, John showed his true and withholding self. John never disputed this characterization, even when encouraged to address it. Martha felt she had been duped. John felt guilty and lost. He did not know if he could change and become the husband Martha wanted. Each in their own way searched for meaning as they tried to enrich their relationship.

When I first saw them, their relationship was on the verge of breaking up. When I stopped seeing them, they believed their relationship had significantly improved. Martha and John never achieved the ideal of marital happiness she had hoped for. John continued to doubt that he could make Martha happy. He struggled with whether or not to stay in the marriage. He then made a commitment to stay and work on sharing more of himself. Eventually, all of the remaining children left home for college. Martha saw to it that all of her daughters had a college education and a good start in life. Upon last contact with the family, all of the women were engaged in professional careers. John continued in his profession.

Redeeming Time by Tapping Spiritual Resources

Depth of meaning is developed when we learn from suffering and come to a new recognition of ourselves as caring and resourceful beings. This recognition often grows in opposition to how we have been defined and treated by others, especially those others who aim to control or serve to diminish our self-understandings. But recognition alone is not enough. We must go further and draw from our suffering profound lessons about life. We must criticize the structures that dominate us from without and from within. Spiritual discernment and criticism are preconditions for transforming the forces that oppress us. Our lives can be dominated by certain inner forces or strivings, and dominated by certain outer, social forces.

We must act justly and with compassion as ways to respond to suffering and create new modes of being. Acts of justice and compassion are the drops of living water that build up and can become an effective force for change. In this light, it is important to note what the nurse assistant did. As we will see, her acts were the drops of experience that became a stream of compassion in a situation of oppression and illness. Her acts aided Martha's recovery. From a certain intellectual standpoint, compassion as a response to suffering appears to lack rigor. It may appear as trivial, overly emotional, and unsophisticated. The nurse assistant appears to have blurred certain limits and crossed certain boundaries by staying with Martha after work hours. To blur boundaries is risky.[4] It can get one into trouble. This act of bonding with Martha could be construed by administration as unprofessional and codependent conduct. However, as we shall see, we can learn beneficial lessons from this nurse assistant about tapping spiritual resources.

Our secular world is lacking in wisdom and courage about the making and sustaining of bonds of affection over time. As bell hooks observed, "Postmodern culture with its decentered subject can be the space where ties are severed or it can provide the occasion for new and varied forms of bonding."[5] Postmodernism, especially in the form of managed care, is characterized by efficiency, cost-effectiveness, detachment; a loss of historical memory, sense of community, neighborhood, and tradition; and dismantling of identities. This sense of loss at the level of culture is also epitomized in Martha's experience. It is important, then, to note what the nurse assistant did. As a lay person, this nurse assistant teaches us something important about responding to suffering, caring for others, and tapping spiritual resources. She built a bridge to hope over waves of despair. Through small acts of kindness and repetition, she helped to create streams of compassion that enabled change in the course of Martha's illness. In the process, she connects us to the past and provides certain clues about how to act in future situations despairing of hope.

How did the nurse assistant do all of this? How did she connect us with the past, help to develop depth of meaning, reflexivity, and a sense of agency? Was it all her doing? Timing was a factor in developing reflexivity, a sense of agency, and depth of meaning. We can name three emphases in her action that contributed to the development of depth of meaning, reflexivity, and a sense of agency. They are *outreach, inreach,* and *the communication of intrinsic worth.* I believe these emphases were instrumental in Martha's recovery and are expressions of African American spirituality.

African American spirituality is an admixture of non-Western and Western influences. It has roots in traditional African beliefs and practices and in Western Christianity, especially as it took shape in the Americas and the Caribbean. Central to all African religious beliefs is the idea of the Supreme Being and the interrelatedness of all things. This includes a belief in the spirit world, and the idea that the Divine Spirit works in and through and beyond human activity. This means the divine intent operates in outreach efforts, it elicits emotional responses, and communicates a sense of intrinsic worth. African American spirituality emerged in response to conditions of dehumanization with the counterexperience of the total acceptance of the self by God. This experience provides moral challenge and spiritual resistance to dehumanizing conditions. It would be consistent with African American spirituality, then, for Martha to believe that in this time of crisis, the nurse assistant was an emissary of the Divine Spirit, and that the special place at night where they met was imbued with divine intent.[6] The idea that the divine intent operates in history and through human agency and firmly situated in the midst of everyday activity is characteristic of African American spirituality.[7]

A central theme in African American spirituality is agape love. It is the radical idea that God sides with the oppressed and works for their freedom; and there is nothing that can separate the believer from the love of God. This means that God is continuously at work as liberating and transforming presence in everything. The sufferer, then, is not merely a victim, but also a participant and resource in a transforming process. The appropriate response to God's love, then, is manifest as an ethical norm that motivates the sufferer to also reach out to other sufferers and extend the process of liberation and transformation. This ethical norm of agape love further means that in African American spirituality words and actions are not separated, but are kept together. One could see this norm operating in the civil rights movement of the 1960s as black civil rights activists and their supporters risked their lives to register disenfranchised black voters. This same norm is at work in the relationship between the nurse assistant and Martha. These three emphases of African American spirituality (outreach, inreach, communication of value or intrinsic worth) will illustrate how reflexivity, sense of agency, and depth of meaning were achieved. They link Martha's experience and the nurse assistant with what is central in African American spiritual traditions.

Outreach

We know very little about the nurse assistant. We can only speculate about why she reached out to Martha. She was a member of a black church and shared the church's belief about God's love. She knew the Scriptures and the spirituals. She knew how to express these and saw an opportunity to do so. Perhaps, then, the nurse assistant was engaged in self-reflexive thinking when she first noticed Martha and thought about reaching out to her. Reflexive thinking is a form of empathy. It is the capacity to be imaginatively engaged in a relationship and to anticipate the effects of the act, and our cocreative response. Through reflexive thinking, the nurse assistant anticipated that if she did reach out, Martha might not respond. Why should she? Martha had experienced betrayal and abandonment, shame, hurt, anger, isolation, and despair. But Martha would respond in a manner that reflected the crosscurrents that were moving beneath the surface of her life.

The nurse assistant's sense of agency was expressed when she acted on her ideas. Her sense of agency and reaching out became a basis for the emergence of a new experience. By taking the initiative and reaching out, the nurse assistant became a channel for the faith community's belief in God's love. She enabled something to happen. A relationship was in the making. She was acting on her ideas and doing for Martha what she would want Martha to do for her had the situation been reversed. At this point, Martha was in despair and unable to articulate her deepest needs.

In the act of reaching out was the potential for the development of depth of meaning, both in the nurse assistant and in Martha. The nurse assistant would go beyond the call of duty and become engaged in a relationship that would stimulate Martha's desire to live again. The nurse assistant would develop depth of meaning through acts of faithfulness in that each night she would come at a regular time.

The nurse assistant was faithful in that she was consistent. She moved physically close—i.e., would sit at Martha's bedside, talk to her, and softly hum a spiritual. It could have been difficult at first when the nurse assistant began reaching out. Martha could have resisted the nurse assistant's efforts. She could have cursed her and told her to go away. Martha could have escaped into sleep. She could have continued her refusal of food. She could have kept silent and remained unresponsive.

True, the nurse assistant had an entrance through her regular duties. But why this nurse assistant, and why was she going beyond the call of duty? She had already put in a full evening's work. She had earned her pay. It was late. It was night and time to go home. But she remained and was consistent even though there was no guarantee that Martha wanted this or would respond. After all, she had "given up." Had Martha already made that decision to "give up" in that inner world where for us the great issues of our lives are determined? By reaching out, the nurse assistant expressed an emphasis of African American spirituality.

Inreach

Inreach is the intuitive sense that one somehow understands the unspoken need and deep spiritual sighs of another. The Apostle Paul said there are some sighs that are too deep for words (Romans 8:26) Inreach is able to use that sense of connection to stimulate hope. Hence, outreach, through physical closeness, while necessary, is not sufficient to counter despair in someone with a diagnosis of a fatal illness. Martha's cancer meant that she was dying. The cancer had become a symbol for her losing struggle to find fulfillment in life. Receiving the news of a fatal illness can be devastating. One's inner world, sense of priorities, and style of life can change dramatically as one becomes preoccupied by the illness. A sense of agency is lost. We may assume that the nurse assistant was familiar with the dynamic of despair that accompanies a patient's sense of loss of control.

Self-reflexive thinking was being expressed when the nurse assistant responded to the meaning of the illness. "Inreach" is another basis for the emergence of something new or transformative in experience. As she reached out to Martha, something was being called out in her as well. African Americans are keen observers and respond to people's nonverbal as well as verbal behaviors. They internalize the nonverbal responses from others long before they are able to talk about them.[8] The nurse assistant saw something in Martha that she could connect with. In order to find that something, she had to have been looking for it. I do not know what it was. Maybe the name for it is hope. Hope may be defined as receptive responses to acts of care. Hope anticipates redemption, the possibility that one can cope and have control, and find fulfillment in caring relationships. Hope is a strong emotion, and emotions play a significant role in African American spirituality. It may be thought of as the soul's barometer giving indications of its inner movement. The opposite of hope is apathy, despair, and nihilism—i.e., the rejection of guiding principles and the belief that all of life is meaningless, or unredeemable.

How was the nurse assistant's sense of agency expressed? Agency means to have the capacity and freedom to help shape the course of events. A sense of agency was expressed in the nurse assistant's choice of activity.

We may ask, what is distinctively African American about these activities? Would not this description fit the situation of any woman who has been abused, regardless of race or ethnicity? We remember that the wider context in which this relationship unfolds is the American mainstream. There Martha's value and the value of the black nurse assistant are devalued. In this society black people are different and therefore alleged to be innately inferior to whites; or whites are alleged to be naturally superior to blacks. Either way, a pathological belief in white supremacy is supported, has been institutionalized, and is an enduring feature of American society. It is frequently backed by scientific racism, which finds support in major white universities in the United States and elsewhere. Scientific racism is based on IQ and genetic measures. White researchers assert that black people are genetically deficient. This view is called the Genetically Deficient Model (Shuey, 1966; Jensen, 1969; Herrnstein, 1971; Shockley, 1972; Rushton, 1989; Brand, 1996). No one can live in a racist society for long without being affected by such institutionalized beliefs. As members of society, I assume that both Martha and the nurse assistant have been affected by such beliefs and have experienced the difficulties of being black in a racist society. We remember, for example, Martha's depiction of the white judge who referred to her in stereotypical fashion as "demanding" and vindictive. In addition, many black women are raised to not trust other black women and are frequently measured by the beauty standards of white women.[9] If these things are true, Martha's experiences here are not identical with those of "any" abused woman. What is distinctly African American about this encounter between Martha and the nurse assistant is that they are *black,* and therefore must struggle against racism if they wish to survive. They are *female,* and therefore must defend themselves against expressions of male power in its white and black manifestations. True, sexist attitudes and practices affect all women, but race and ethnicity make a difference. Black women's distress from sexism is aggravated and reinforced by institutional racism. Over the years my biological sisters have shared their bitterness about racism in the workplace when white women were given privileges denied them and promoted to posts for which they (my sisters) were positioned.

My sister, Geraldine, said, "There is a sisterhood at work, but it works for white women only." Black women are frequently *isolated, unsupported, and misunderstood* when they experience success or show that they are strong and brave. Martha and the nurse assistant drew upon African American spiritual resources and transcended cultural lessons of distrust, made new connections, and affirmed one another.

A sense of agency was expressed in the nurse assistant's presence night after night. She hummed familiar songs, read Scripture, and prayed. In so doing she and Martha enacted a historical and spiritual tradition that has created meaning and given hope in the midst of black suffering. Black worship experiences continue to reflect the experience of common suffering. The language of the spiritual helped to give meaning to Martha's suffering. It provided a context for interpreting the activity of the nurse assistant. Through these repeated acts, the nurse assistant was able to reach in and touch something of value in Martha.

The dimension of depth was expressed when Martha became self-reflexive and caught a glimpse of herself as a valued person through the faithful efforts of the nurse assistant. Maybe it was the regularity of the assistant's visits that countered Martha's experience of abandonment. Martha came to trust the nurse assistant and in time offered her self through talk. Maybe it was the humming of spirituals that stirred something familiar and meaningful in Martha. Perhaps it was all of these, in combination. Whatever it was, the nurse assistant reached inward and creatively drew from her own spiritual depths. This movement answered a need within Martha. The joining of their efforts gave rise to hope. By reaching in, the nurse assistant expressed an emphasis of African American spirituality. Together their drops of experience formed a stream of compassion and the heavy burdens of Martha's life were transported from despair to hope.

Communication of Value or Intrinsic Worth

African American spirituality is marked by a belief in the intrinsic worth of all human beings. We are made in the image of God, and the divine intent struggles against evil forces and works for their transformation. The nurse assistant knew that Martha was refusing to eat her food. Reflecting on her time in the hospital, Martha said that her plan was to starve herself to death by refusing to eat. Indeed, Martha was in the process of starving herself to death as her weight dropped from 140 pounds to around 97 pounds. The nurse assistant surmised that Martha had given up. She may have surmised from reflecting on previous experience that when patients lose control through illness, they lose hope. When they lose hope, they also lose a sense of self-worth. She believed that her regular visits and special manner of caring could counter Martha's multiple sense of loss. She imagined that her efforts would communicate a sense of Martha's intrinsic value.

The nurse assistant began her communications with Martha by talking to her, and by showing that she cared. Her efforts proved effective and conveyed to Martha that she still had choices and could make things happen, rather than having things happen to her.

Martha had noted that the nurse assistant was not merely going about her assigned duties. Something more was going on here. Martha had not requested this special attention, but it was being offered freely, with care, and at a time when Martha was bereft of a sense of self-esteem and personal potency. The nurse assistant's sense of timing was important. Her gestures stood out in sharp contrast to Martha's own life experience of betrayal and abandonment. The nurse assistant could not have known the troubled details of Martha's personal history. She was not intentionally acting in response to the facts of Martha's life. The nurse assistant was responding to the woman before her whom she had come to care about without knowing the details.

The dimension of depth was conveyed in that the nurse assistant was able to communicate to Martha this spiritual emphasis of unconditional acceptance and intrinsic worth that seemed to contradict the objective facts of Martha's life. It went beyond her own self-assessment. The nurse assistant was able to communicate care and respect for Martha through words and deeds. In this way she expressed an emphasis of African American spirituality.

In some manner this nurse assistant, through the sharing of her own faith, communicated to Martha the caring presence of God, the healing ministry of Jesus, and the support of community. These are the lessons we can learn from the nurse assistant about tapping spiritual resources. Outreach, inreach, and the communication of value or intrinsic worth are characteristic emphases in African American spirituality.

When I first met with Martha, she told me this story and expressed her profound gratitude for this nurse assistant who showed up just in time and without explanation. She gave Martha reason to hope, and hope is an essential element in recovery. Martha said, "She is the reason that I am alive today." Not just living, but "alive!"

In these three overlapping and interwoven emphases, depth of meaning, reflexivity, and sense of agency were developed in the context of Martha's suffering and experience with cancer. These three African American spiritual emphases should not be construed in linear fashion as steps. The nurse assistant did not follow a fixed procedure that moved her from step one through step three. Rather, there was a widening and deepening of the river. Martha and the nurse assistant represent the coming together of two streams of experience, where the isolation of Martha was overcome and the nurse assistant's capacity to care was deepened and given added meaning. Their coming together constituted a stream wider than the separate individuals. They participated in a reciprocal process, a flowing backward and forward where meaning was developed and hope came alive. Together they contribute to the river's flow. At the same time, the river would enrich the meaning of African American spirituality, and the unique identities of Martha and the nurse assistant as they reflect on this experience and tell their story in the new communities they help to create.

> This wider life that emerges through the loving relationship between selves does not swallow up individuals, blurring their identities and concerns. It is not an undifferentiated whole that obliterates individuality. On the contrary, the wider life created by love constitutes a community of persons. In a community, persons retain their identity, and they also share a commitment to the continued well-being of the relational life uniting them.[10]

Their stories will join with the stories of others who have experienced care and the overcoming of despair. In the words of John's epistle, "We know that we have passed [from death to life] because we love one another. Whoever does not love abides in death." (1 John 3:14) By way of contrast with T. S. Eliot, time past and time present is redeemed by love in time future.

The three spiritual emphases mentioned above should not be construed as the methodology for the deepening of meaning. They were shared as parts of an identifiable process that proved effective in this situation. At the time, it was a bridge over waves of despair that could have taken Martha under. A goal of pastoral care with African Americans, indeed with all individuals and families, is to help them to find the riverbank of their experience that will enable their spiritual lives to touch the past, grow, and deepen—as they learn to stem the tide in times of suffering; to inspire hope, and enable them to achieve a sense of self-efficacy or agency in the context of oppression.

Summary and Conclusion

The purpose of this chapter was to show how the river metaphor can aid the interpretation of a pastoral care situation. Depth of meaning, reflexivity, and sense of agency were the key interpretive principles. Rather than focusing on my work as a therapist with Martha, I chose instead to share the story Martha told of her life-changing experience with the nurse assistant. In the process of listening to Martha's story, I came to appreciate the story within the story, the story about the nurse assistant. That story within a story is about how a lay person, moved by the currents of her own life, became the river's bank for Martha. She provided the higher ground amidst the rising tide of troubles that could take Martha's life.

The nurse assistant became the real and effective pastoral caregiver. In the context of racism, and in a life-threatening illness, through her loving visits, she reaffirmed Martha's worth, while simultaneously eliciting (or welcoming) from her a response to living. If we use the nurse assistant as a model, then we are directed to a central theme in African American spirituality, namely, agape love. It was the basis for tapping streams of meaning through

99

singing spirituals and hymns, and reading Scripture even though she did not know whether Martha would accept these offerings.

It is against the background of black suffering that black spiritual experience is best understood. African American spirituality developed historically as a multifarious response to human suffering. It produced prayer traditions, self-help programs, scriptural interpretation, the shout and various states of ecstasy, sorrow songs, rituals, and the spirituals. African American spirituality was a way to redefine one's situation, transcend dehumanizing conditions, and affirm God, self and others while facing cruel oppression. The bedrock of black spirituality is the shared conviction that God is a God who sees the oppression of people, hears their groans, and promises to deliver them. It is the basis for fashioning meaning and hope in the midst of cruel suffering. This is what gave birth to the spirituals. It is this perspective that helps us see that Martha and the nurse assistant were drawing on a tradition with emphases that are deep and rich and transgenerational. African American spirituality continues to bring healing, comfort, inspiration, hope, faith, and fresh vision to thousands in their time of suffering. Because African American spirituality enables people to mature as they draw from their suffering profound lessons about human life, it must be regarded as an indispensable resource for personal and social transformation.

Martha could depend on the nurse assistant's visits, whose regularity reinforced cycles of meaning. Martha's care did not reply on complex interpretations of her condition. But it did depend primarily on a giving of self—the only words, at times, being those of spiritual songs and Scripture. The timing was ripe for the power of the word to be enhanced by the context through which the word was given.

~

6

> *Since we know that African-Americans are a displaced,*
> *exilic people, it should be understood that we suffer*
> *the pain of estrangement and alienation in all its*
> *multiple manifestations. And as the conditions of life*
> *worsen materially and spiritually within the context*
> *of postmodernism, it does not seem surprising that*
> *underclass black people feel more acutely this contem-*
> *porary anguish and despair. Again, I do not think it*
> *useful to simply name this nihilism and let it go at*
> *that, to be passively terrorized by it, we have to find*
> *and talk about the ways we critically intervene,*
> *to provide hope, to offer strategies of transformation.*
>
> bell hooks, *Yearning*

What prepares caregivers to critically intervene, provide hope, and offer strategies of transformation with displaced, exilic people, as a captured group who have been uprooted from their land of origin, enslaved, and transported to a foreign country, where they continued to be targets of hostility and discrimination? What do caregivers need to know, be, or learn, in order to tap the spiritual resources of African American family members who turn to them for help?

In this chapter I briefly make the point that the work of today's therapist belongs to an ancient tradition of healers and a continuous stream of experience that is much wider and deeper than the current secular spirit of society tends to acknowledge. Then I reflect on modern-day training experiences and the questions that emerge.

Ancient healers such as witch doctors, medicine men and women, faith healers, or shamans critically intervened in the social context to provide hope and offer strategies of transformation. They shared a common belief that the Spirit of the Divine Other reality permeated everyday life, and sought to meld spiritual and material resources in their solution to an existential crisis. Expressions of such beliefs and practices varied from culture to culture and over time. The idea of spiritual and material resources working together has been eclipsed in secular society. Yet human experience is too deep and wide, and expressions of the human spirit are too rich and varied, to limit our understanding of them to one epoch. There may be some wisdom in recollecting that the tapping of spiritual resources is an ancient and enduring quest of the human spirit. Ancient healers tapped spiritual resources when they sought to keep hope alive and counter negative emotions such as anxiety, depression, despair, and hopelessness. They did this by evoking healing powers through ritual and ceremonies, and they were usually successful if they were able to break through the help seekers' isolation, demonstrate that others cared about them, and empower the help seekers to help themselves.[1] How is hope and a sense of the spirit configured in secular settings today?

Brenda McHugh, Neil Dawson, and Betty Gray are contemporaries who work with marginalized families and seek to intervene in a social context, provide hope, and offer strategies for change. They are educators based in Britain who trained as family therapists and work with parents and their children within the two most significant learning contexts for a child, namely, school and family. The children are between ages 5 and 16, and have been referred because of severe behavioral or learning difficulties. These children experience isolation and have sometimes been referred to as "aggressive, abusive, violent, destructive, withdrawn, negative, rejecting and often frightening to deal with."[2] Their parents have sometimes been experienced as hostile, rejecting, apparently uncaring, violent, depressed, helpless, abusive or generally difficult to deal with."[3] McHugh, Dawson, and Gray intervene in a seemingly hopeless situation, work closely with the school and family to establish communication and to overcome isolation and a sense of helplessness. They explain their approach:

> When a child is referred to us at the Marlborough Family Service Education Unit, the message from teachers in school is usually: "We've used all our expertise to try to help this child but nothing makes any difference." We always talk to our colleagues to find out what has been tried at school but make a general assumption that before calling in an agency such as ours, many things will inevitably have been tried by a child's teacher(s). The job that we are asked to do is to investigate the child's life outside the school and to see if resources can be found which can help alleviate the situation for the child in school. This is consistent with the theoretical framework we have learned since working at the Marlborough Family Service, a psychiatric department of the Middlesex Hospital based in an old house in St John's Wood. Our work is based on a "Family Systems" approach which focuses on the family as the key to problems people have, but also the key to potential solutions to the same problems.[4]

McHugh, Dawson, and Gray usually have their first meeting with the family in their home and aim to give some hope that things can change for the better.[5] In addition, they provide a classroom at the Marlborough Family Service Education Unit where parents can participate in their child's learning. The classroom is also a social context for the parents to share parenting difficulties with one another. This is important because "a common factor in most of the families we see is social isolation within the community. Families with children with behavioural problems are not very popular in the neighbourhood."[6] When families meet at the Educational Unit, they share not only their difficulties, but also solutions. Families encourage and give reassurance to each other. This way of working is unconventional in that McHugh, Dawson, and Gray combine the roles of teacher and family therapist, using family systems principles to intervene in the home, in the school, and in the classroom that they provide at the Education Unit. There is no standard way to describe their role. Much of what they do bridges the role of teacher, family therapist, and social worker. "As teachers we are able to observe the child's difficulties at first hand. Our aim then is to switch roles and to talk with the family to discuss what function the child's behaviour might have for the family as a whole. Family tasks and interventions are then made to try to bring about a change in the whole family."[7]

McHugh, Dawson, and Gray's work demonstrates the importance of context. They intervene in the social context of the child and demonstrate the importance of systemic work. They work with children from different social, cultural, and ethnic backgrounds and communicate care and hope to families who have been isolated, exiled, and labeled as hostile or frightening. They communicate hope by collaborating with family members as partners in the solution to their problems and by negotiating with them about where the first meeting should be held and who should attend. As a result, family members feel respected and valued. McHugh, Dawson, and Gray communicate care by empowering both parent and child to make difficult but desirable changes. While spirituality is not an explicit part of their work, it is implicit in their manner of working with people. Theology and spirituality are not part of their professional training, but still they seek consultation on how to address these issues as they arise in their work with families. In this light, what do today's caregivers need to know about tapping into the spiritual resources of African American and other families?

A black woman caregiver-in-training from East Africa once asked me, "Do you have to be a believer in any particular religion before you can help a family with their religious beliefs? Indigenous forms of religion are springing up all over Africa. I see them as a problem. How can I relate to this phenomenon and learn to positively value it?" Indeed, how does one learn to relate to and see the good in unfamiliar religious and/or spiritual experiences that may run counter to one's own values and beliefs?

Training to be a caregiver is a lifelong learning, unlearning, and new learning process about providing hope amidst despair and offering strategies and resources that lead to transformation possibilities. There are signs of a coming together of two streams of therapeutic traditions that have previously followed separate paths. On one hand, the field of marriage and family therapy has shown increased interest in spirituality and the spiritual beliefs of families.[8] On the other hand, pastoral counselors and theologians have recognized and applied the contributions of family therapy in situations requiring pastoral care.[9] But the training of these caregivers may not enable them to tap and mobilize cultural resources. They may not know how to relate their learning or training to transformational possibilities in the wider social system. McHugh, Dawson, and Gray suggest that knowledge and skills that were developed to relieve specific situations of human suffering can be fashioned to critically intervene in the wider social system. However, caregivers need to develop awareness, knowledge, and skill in combining systemic intervention and spirituality in training programs. This can be part of the caregiver's preparation.

A few months ago, I was asked to give a lecture to a group of caregivers-in-training. We gathered in a large classroom at a university. My lecture was to address how family therapy principles could apply to the wider social system. The students had already been introduced to the basic concepts of family therapy through lectures, reading, and discussion. They came mostly from backgrounds in social work, psychology, and psychiatry. I identified several key principles of structural family therapy: joining, context, boundaries, reframing and restructuring, and systems thinking. I set these principles within the setting of my street and community ministry at the First Baptist Church of Worcester, Massachusetts. My street ministry with young people, black and poor families, the police, courts, prisons, schools, social welfare departments, industry and religious institutions represented involvement with a wider society. What these caregivers needed to know, I thought, is that family therapy principles, knowledge, and skills that were developed to relieve specific situations of human suffering could be related to intervention strategies in the wider social system.[10]

When I was minister-to-the-community and on staff at the First Baptist Church of Worcester, Massachusetts, I took the time to visit industry and the personnel managers of several companies. On one hand, I was able to form a working relationship with several personnel managers and interpreted to them the nature of my work, which was to find employment for the so-called hard-core unemployed. On the other hand, I spent time in the neighborhood, on street corners, in barrooms, on the playgrounds, in churches, the courts, city jails, and community or neighborhood centers, and I made home visits, where I was likely to meet and get to know unemployed men and women. Where a pastoral or therapeutic relationship could be established, and when the timing was right, I was able to join those who were looking for work with someone who had a job opening that paid better than entry-level wages. Through continued home visits, pastoral work, and follow-up work, I was able to learn more about the strengths of the people with whom I worked. I responded to specific situations of suffering and grief when tragedy occurred. I also learned about subtle dynamics of class, race, and gender issues related to unemployment in my community. I learned to anticipate difficulties and work with individuals, family members, and employers when problems arose in the workplace. One young man—I will call him Fred—would frequently take up his position on a street corner opposite my apartment. Fred was there every day by 12 noon with brown bag and bottle. Soon he was joined by others, who shared the contents of his brown bag. Whenever I passed or came into view, I would greet the brothers, and they would respond, "hello, Rev." I worked closely with Fred's younger siblings and mother. One day, Fred approached and asked if I could help him find a job. I told him I would. I called a personnel manager of a major company where I had established a relationship. An appointment for a job interview was set. Fred was nervous and asked if I would accompany him. The next day we drove to the interview. Fred was offered a job. With my encouragement, the personnel manager connected Fred with a company-sponsored Alcoholics Anonymous program. With Fred's permission, I informed his family of what was going on and asked for their encouragement and support. I also informed the bartender at the tavern where Fred hung out and asked for his support of Fred's new direction. This pattern of providing a bridge between young men on the street, social services, and employment multiplied. By intervening in this way in a wider social system where unemployment was high, I was able to provide hope and offer strategies for change. This was a first step toward organizing the community and its leaders to build supportive networks, mobilize cultural resources, and address problems of unemployment. I worked with neighbourhood residents, ministers, and others who were willing to help build networks of support. A sense of helplessness or despair that can come from prolonged periods of unemployment can be countered when jobs and training are provided, and when it is demonstrated that others care. By joining with industry, understanding and respecting their needs and work ethic, I was able to meet and join with those who were looking for work and help prepare them for successful employment. In this way I used the strategy of joining, building relationships of respect and trust between people, and made interventions into a wider social system.

After the lecture, a few students, including one of the instructors, responded that they did not see the connection between the principles I had identified, how they applied to all these other institutions, and family therapy. There were too many levels involved—personal, family, the workplace, community agencies, religion, and so on. Another instructor thought the ideas were clear and that the connections suggested some new directions. As people filed out of the room, there were four or five who hung back. When there were only a few people left, they approached and identified themselves as clergy from several different denominations. They wanted to thank me for a lecture that showed them connections between family therapy concepts, people who have been marginalized, community resources, the ministry of the church, and the wider social system. One priest from East Africa, in particular, said, "That was most helpful. I did not know these ideas could be put together like that. I came to this program hoping they could. You showed me that it was possible."

On the one hand, ideas that linked family therapy principles (such as joining, context, boundary, reframing, restructuring and systems thinking) to issues relevant within church and society were viewed with great skepticism or dismissed out of hand by some students. On the other hand, these ideas were met with great appreciation by another group of students.

I did not have a follow-up contact with these students. Therefore, I can only speculate about the difference between the group who saw connections between family therapy ideas and the wider social system, and the group who did not. I believe that age and experience may have been factors distinguishing the two groups of students. The clergy who were receiving training as family therapists appeared to be slightly older. They had been practicing as clergy and were already leaders in their various faith communities. The other students appeared younger, with less life experience. They may have been training for their first professional post. The majority of the students were white, a very few were Asian, and one or two were black or African. The clergy in their pastoral role would naturally be exposed to family situations such as premarital and marital counseling, the baptism of children, domestic violence, separation or divorce counseling; calling on families at the time of births, deaths, or grieving; officiating at burial and memorial services, etc. Clergy are involved with families throughout the life cycle and family members frequently turn to their ministers during times of crisis. Many areas of family life bring clergy into contact with different or unfamiliar problems. They must take risks, go against conventional wisdom, and take unorthodox positions by standing with those who are marginalized, or isolated, or whom society has condemned. Often contacts with family members involve contact with housing, health, education, economic, and legal institutions in the wider community. For example, one socially active pastor put it this way:

> I have watched families struggle with an assortment of devastating problems. I have shared the pain of families in which members have been accused of or convicted of theft, drug addiction, prostitution, rape, and murder. I have been involved with homeless families who have been so desperate for a place to live that squatting in abandoned houses was their only recourse. I have witnessed elderly persons lose all sense of autonomy because of homelessness, illness, and loneliness. I have witnessed a remarkable fact—for these persons the church has been the central au-

thenticating reality in their lives. When the world has so often been willing to say only "no" to these people, the church has said "yes." For black people the church has been the one place where they have been able to experience unconditional positive regard.[11]

When a family member turns to the pastor for help, the pastor is challenged to interpret what is going on in personal lives, the working of the mainstream, family and faith resources. Such clergy may also be politically active, and understand the biblical connections between religious faith and social transformation. In various ways they may seek to relate the spiritual world to the world of everyday family life, where people sometimes suffer. Whether Methodist, Baptist, or Catholic, they can draw on church traditions and teachings that prepare them to take risks, face otherness, and link personal piety and prophetic witness.

Students who do not have this background and are nurtured in traditions that do not connect religious faith and social activism would have more difficulty with my presentation. They would not be looking for the connections I was making. Nor would they necessarily be interested in influencing the spirit world or learning to tap spiritual resources as a part of family therapy thinking. If religion or spirituality is understood in private terms, or seen as irrelevant to social worlds, or as a source of pathology, a positive connection would not be made between faith and social action. It would not be linked to personal and social transformation. Younger, mostly white students may not see themselves working with black or other ethnic minority families. They may not anticipate, and therefore are not preparing for, working in ethnic minority communities on one hand, or challenging institutional racism in the majority community on the other. To do so would involve them in challenging the status quo of race and power relations in their places of employment, and expose them to risks they can choose to avoid.

Among the groups of students being trained as family therapists, the dichotomy between those who see a connection and those who do not leads to new questions. What is required to train caregivers to critically intervene, provide hope, and offer strategies of transformation with isolated, marginalized, or displaced exilic people? How can certain principles be developed in the field of family therapy to *enhance* the church's ministry with African American families in the context of the wider society? How can the culture of black churches, and its manner of reaching out to despairing souls, inform the work of family therapists? How does black church culture construct or inspire hope in the face of despair? How can caregivers learn to positively access spiritual resources within the life of the family? Do they need to believe the same things that African American family members believe in order to help? How can they value the meaning of religious experiences in the life of black families, especially where religious faith is valued by family members? What prepares caregivers to critically intervene, provide hope, and offer strategies of transformation is a spiritual and intellectual openness to new and demanding experiences; a maturing relationship with an exemplary teacher, trainer, or guide; and a sense of emptiness about what one knows or a willingness to be filled and learn from mistakes or perceived failure.

~

7

WHAT THERAPISTS IN TRAINING NEED TO KNOW

> *In everlasting memory of the anguish of our ancestors.*
> *May those who died rest in peace. May those who*
> *return find their roots. May humanity never again*
> *perpetrate such injustice against humanity. We, the*
> *living, vow to uphold this.*
>
> A small sign by the exit of a former
slave quarter, Ghana
The Independent, Sunday, 5 May, 1996

> *How can any white person do family therapy with*
> *people who have been the subject of colonialism with*
> *all the negative effects of colonial domination on the*
> *cultures and day to day lives of colonised people?*
> *All that might be done in a therapeutic situation*
> *must . . . be tainted with further tinges of colonialism.*
> *Thus, is it possible ever for our theories and the*
> *practice through which those theories are lived out*
> *to be anything more than further extensions of the*
> *colonialist position?*
>
> W. Peter Lang, Human Systems

In 1995 the result of an important empirical study demonstrating the efficacy of marriage and family therapy (MFT) training and supervision was reported.[1] A panel of experts were selected because of their expertise in training and supervision in accredited MFT master's, doctoral, or other postgraduate degree programs. The panelists were fairly evenly divided between males and females. They were almost exclusively white, and the majority had achieved a doctoral degree of some kind. The purpose of the study was to identify the important variables that will lay the foundation for a comprehensive model of MFT supervision. The study focused on three categories of variables: (1) supervisor variables, (2) supervisee variables, and (3) contextual or setting variables.

This study is important because it contributes to the criteria for accrediting training programs and evaluating standards for supervision. At the same time, it is limited in that it does not reflect the concerns of a racially diverse population. The context for therapy supervision is limited to clinics, centers, and other sites where video equipment, one-way mirrors, and reflecting teams are used. These features, while very useful for some segments of the population, may be culturally inappropriate for others. We are led to the following questions: How will such foundational knowledge include and be sensitive toward people from cultures and ethnic groups other than white middle class professionals? What will prevent theory and practice from being anything more than further extensions of colonialism?

Sue and Sue address a similar question and have identified skills and characteristics of the effective cross-cultural counselor.[2] First, such a counselor "is able to relate to minority-group experiences and has knowledge of cultural and class factors." The skilful cross-cultural counselor is able to recognize differences between ethnic minority groups as well as differences within ethnic groups. Second, such a counselor will have a variety of approaches and skills in her or his repertoire, since no one approach will be applicable to different ethnic minority groups, or to the changing circumstances of members of the same ethnic group over time. Third, the skilful cross-cultural counselor continues to examine her or his own values, assumptions, and experiences with different racial or ethnic groups, and examines the cultural assumptions and values that underlie various schools of counseling.

These are important skills and characteristics to be actively developed. But what makes the counselor "able" or ready to relate in these ways in the first place? Several characteristics seem especially important. They are warmth and sincerity combined with skill and experience. The skilful therapist must be comfortable within her or himself and must communicate warmth and acceptance of African American family members. If the therapist communicates discomfort, defensiveness, arrogance, or an "I know best" attitude, then the therapist will succeed in further extending the colonialist position. He or she will not be able to help. The skilful therapist will show curiosity and a willingness to explore the contributions of family members—and deftness enough to find value in such contributions. Second, he or she will be familiar with and able to utilize African American cultural resources and strengths while addressing perceived weaknesses. He or she will be aware of the role of white history, including the history of white supremacy in the United States. The skilful white counselor will continue to examine his or her own experience of being socialized in a racist society and how his or her experience of being white affects therapeutic interventions, the goals of therapy, and the therapeutic relationship with African America families.

In this chapter I continue the focus on the training of family therapists and what they need to know. Specifically, I suggest four interrelated areas for tapping spiritual resources in African American families. They are: (1) the importance of African American religious institutions, their meaning and symbolism; (2) caregivers' attitudes and beliefs; (3) the context of therapy; and (4) common ground for family therapists and pastoral counselors.

The Importance of African American Religious Institutions

Black religious institutions are the repositories of the community's spiritual legacy. Their resources need to be tapped. Historically, the black church is the oldest and most durable institution providing cohesion and hope among the elect in African American communities. ("The elect" is a term used in African American religious communities to refer to those who understand themselves to be saved from sin and/or chosen by God and community to lead exemplar religious lives.) Behind black church cultures in the United States are African worldviews and spiritual traditions, the invisible institution called slave religion, and traditions of black folk culture, which include, but are not limited to, music and the arts. We cannot review those traditions here,[3] but they help to constitute the deep river of African American spirituality. African American spirituality has its origins in Africa and finds expression wherever African descendants are gathered in large numbers and where black culture has flourished in parts of the United States, Brazil, Haiti, the British West Indies, the Virgin Islands, other areas of the Caribbean, and parts of the United Kingdom.

Black or African American religious cultures, as resources to be tapped, have not often been appreciated in professional family therapy circles and training programs. Whether they are regular attenders or not, many African Americans have some church affiliation. Many more African Americans ascribe to some form of spirituality, even if they claim no church or formal religious affiliation. Generally, and with some exceptions, the African American church has reached out to the whole black community. It is primarily a house of prayer. It has also been a gathering place, an educational site, a financial institution, a house of refuge. It has held material and spiritual resources together and "affirms the presence of the spirit world in the daily life of the community."[4] As we shall soon see, it can be thought of as a shamanic community in that through worship, it depicts and dramatizes the existential situation of human suffering, provides hope, and offers resolution.

Today, the family, the church, and the schools are, perhaps, the most important institutions that African Americans have to redress the workings of the social, economic, and political systems that affect their lives. When I grew up in Seattle, Washington, during the 1940s and 1950s, the Mt. Zion Baptist Church provided strong and visible leadership for the black community and for the city. It continues to do so. The church was a gathering place for African American people, indeed for all people who sought refuge from the rising tide of injustice. The pastor, the Reverend Doctor Samuel Berry McKinney, referred to this church as a "beacon light" to men and women "of every color, race, and creed." The church "has provided a haven to many seeking and storm tossed souls in our community."[5]

Meaning and Symbol in African American Religious Institutions

The African American church has been the single most important therapeutic and mental health resource for black people outside the black family.[6] Caregivers can learn how to tap the religious resources of African Americans through participation in black worship services. For example, caregivers can learn what the community of faith values and believes, and how they practice their faith. By participating in a variety of African American (black) worship services, caregivers can catch the spirit and power of a community in ways that words or explanation cannot convey.

I invited a student to attend a service at my church. He had been a therapist for many years, but was not familiar with black worship. After the worship service he simply said, "Wow!" What did he learn? Upon reflection he said he learned the power of spirit in the singing and preaching. He felt a sense of uplift that was missing in his own experiences of worship. What W. E. B. DuBois said of the church music years ago is true today:

> The music of Negro religion is that plaintive rhythmic melody, with its touching minor cadences, which, despite caricature and defilement, still remains the most original and beautiful expression of human life and longing yet born on American soil. Sprung from the African forest, where its counterpart can still be heard, it was adapted, changed, and intensified by the tragic soul-life of the slave, until, under the stress of law and whip, it became the one true expression of a people's sorrow, despair, and hope.[7]

There is a coming together and expression of the people's anguish and hope in black worship. The black church is, as Cheryl Townsend Gilkes observed, a therapeutic community. "It is this articulation of suffering through music and speech which seems to have a major therapeutic function within the Black community."[8] My student observed the choir sing and heard the drums beat until the majority of the people were involved through the rhythmic clapping of hands, swaying of bodies, and shouts. He voiced appreciation for the many opportunities for emotional expression in song, prayer, and in the sermon. He learned firsthand about the therapeutic role of the preacher, who used her body, voice, and intellect to stimulate the hearts and the minds of her listeners. He heard the minister use story after story and metaphor upon metaphor to convey her message. The minister's consistent references were to God and the people, their relationship to one another and change. He saw the people's sincere and spirited responses. The body, emotions, and mind must be engaged in a depiction of the suffering situation; and a new or reaffirmed understanding of one's relationship to God, self, and others must be part of the resolution. Music, story, the articulation of core beliefs, and use of metaphor as well as body movement are important elements of a therapeutic ritual that many African Americans recognize.

This white student was interested in African American spirituality and wanted to know what it had to offer him as a therapist, and how he might participate. Attending a black worship service was an experience of otherness, or difference, yet he was not put off by it. At first, he wondered if he would be accepted. But he risked coming, and after the experience he wanted to learn more. But let us imagine what it would have been like had he been put off by this experience or frightened by it, or if he had seen it as not only different, but pathological as well. If that was the case, then he might not have come. Had he come and been turned off, then it would have been very important to process such an experience with this student. Is it possible to reflect on xenophobia? What could he learn about his experiences that would enable him to make meaningful connections and grow? What beneficial lessons could he draw from his experiences with black people and their culture? How might this enable new awareness of his own religious and cultural traditions? If he was a student who was turned off by the black worship experience and unwilling to learn from it, then he would not be in a position to tap African American resources. He would not gain insight into his own American traditions and would not be able to find common ground between African American cultural experiences and his own. This kind of experience can open trainees to new information about the social matrix of meaning and symbols in their own culture and traditions. Fortunately, my student is interested in taking risks, challenging the boundaries of his knowledge, and discovering new bases for questioning social conventions. He is interested in learning from differentness and integrating awareness of otherness into his own experiences as a therapist. This interest positions him to be more effective in a society of increasing social, ethnic, and cultural diversity. This was important learning for my student and can be for others who seek to draw on the spiritual resources of African Americans. Priest and Keller pointed out, "Therapists have rarely been encouraged to explore the spiritual dimension of their client's lives, even though doing so may enrich the understanding of the metaphors and meanings which inform their existence and, perhaps, their problems."[9]

How will knowledge of African American religious institutions or congregations help therapists to tap spiritual resources of African American families? Knowledge of African American religious institutions and appreciation of their therapeutic value may serve as points of reference for the therapist's work. The members of a congregation, over time, have learned to share one another's emotional, physical, and spiritual burdens. They covenant, sing, dance, shout, pray, worship, raise, educate, and care for children and the elderly, learn to disagree, to trust, hope, and grow together.

They share a belief in the parenthood of God and the kinship of all people. On Easter Sunday, 7 April 1996, a 10-month-old baby boy (Cain) was baptized in a Church of England, where I was worshiping. The family and relatives of the child, and the congregation, vowed to raise the child and care for its spiritual and physical well-being as it grew. Then the priest, a black woman, took the baby from the parents (who were also black) and held it up to the congregation and said, "this is your new family." The congregation was made up of black British, black American, African, Asian, Bangladeshi, Irish, Welsh, and English families. Indeed, the child was being introduced to a new and extended family. The congregation, in its turn, vowed to nurture all of the children in its care. What it means to be a member of such a church family will develop over the years as the child participates and matures. This is an unusual, racially mixed congregation and the idea of covenant is essential to its spiritual legacy.

The covenant is an often overlooked yet important part of black church worship services. In some churches and just before the taking of communion, the congregation stands to read or recite the church covenant. It may begin with words such as, "As members of (name of church), we profess our belief in God." It may end with a pledge to live exemplary lives and to deal justly with all people. The covenant is a statement of the church's core beliefs and practices. It initiates newcomers into the beliefs of the community and provides older members an opportunity to renew their commitments one to another. It provides a statement of the church's mission and provides guidance for spiritual discipline and care. In short, the covenant helps to shape religious identity. Over time, church members form an emotional and spiritual bond that crosses several generations. The congregation's covenant, along with Scripture, serves as a reference point for interpreting the meaning of events. It may provide standards ("Let justice roll down like waters, and righteousness like an ever flowing stream" [Amos 5:24]) or values ("love your neighbor") that the help seeker uses for holding self and others accountable. Striving to live by these ideals is at the heart of church membership, spiritual renewal, and ethical reflection. They help to shape the help seeker's idealized self-image and lay at the heart of the help seeker's system of spiritual values to be tapped.

The congregation may provide what Peter Berger called "the sacred canopy." The sacred canopy is an overarching framework of meaning for interpreting good and evil, life and death, and for assigning meaning to events in life. It is the sacred cosmos that parallels the shaman's magic-religious worldview. A church woman, in therapy, may describe what has happened in her life by evoking the sacred canopy, that is, language that is commonly used and has meaning in her religious community. She may say, in the face of a seemingly insurmountable difficulty, "This is hard and I am not sure I will make it, but with God's help, I can do it. God will make a way somehow. God does not give us any more than we can bear." What would it mean to tap this spiritual proverb in the context of her religious community and its covenant of faith? The caregiver can join with her by showing interest in it. The caregiver can try to understand the meaning of this proverb for the woman's life and close relations. Caregivers can do this without immediately delving into or trying to judge the epistemological status of her statement.

Rather, caregivers may acknowledge that she is part of a community of believers who share this proverb. The caregiver may elicit a variety of interpretations of its meaning. Also, there is an extended community of believers who share her faith. They are in Africa, Brazil, the Caribbean, and elsewhere. To tap this resource is to tap a common spirit found among the descendants of Africa. What then, would it entail to access the various levels of meaning of this proverb and the ways it rings true in her life? By using the help seeker's congregation (sacred canopy) and covenant of faith as points of reference, the therapist may be in a better position to tap the help seeker's context of hope, the deep river of her faith, and enrich the spiritual significance of the language, symbols, imagery, and metaphors that African American families bring to therapy. But therapists will not be able to tap spiritual resources if they trivialize or misunderstand the significance of spiritual resources for self-agency, moral guidance, self-esteem, and mental health of African Americans. This leads us to the therapist's attitudes and beliefs.

The Therapist's Attitudes and Beliefs

Attitudes and beliefs in the wider society impact the counseling process, the client and the therapist. Sue and Sue remind us of the important role of attitudes and beliefs in the therapeutic process, especially as they relate to race and ethnicity and cross-cultural experiences,[10] which includes religious and spiritual experiences. "To say that we have somehow escaped our racist upbringing, that we are not perpetuators of racism, or that the racial climate is improving, is to deny reality. As mental health professionals, we have a personal and professional responsibility to (a) confront, become aware of, and take actions in dealing with our biases, stereotypes, values, and assumptions about human behavior, (b) become aware of the culturally different client's world view, values, biases, and assumptions about human behavior, and (c) develop appropriate help-giving practices, intervention strategies, and structures that take into account the historical, cultural, and environmental experiences/influences of the culturally different client."[11] The current pulls both ways in that these comments are relevant for the client as well as for the therapist. A black female, Muslim trainee identified the importance of belief when she felt terror after a white male counselee talked about his fantasies about black women. She was unprepared for this and did not know how to respond. What were the implications of his comments for her as a black woman, a trainee, and a practicing Muslim? Was she in danger? Fortunately, she was in a training setting with others, where she could work through her feelings of terror.

A white colleague once informed me that she was going to refer a Japanese couple to me for marital counseling. My colleague was treating the wife, who requested marital therapy. My colleague said, "I am not a family therapist, but I know of a very fine family therapist to whom I would like to refer you." The wife seemed interested. I waited for the referral, but it never came. I followed up by asking my colleague what happened. Embarrassed, my colleague said that when the wife was informed that I, the family therapist, was black, she wanted nothing to do with the referral. Her beliefs about and attitude toward black people were strongly negative. She would never consider a black therapist. Attitudes and beliefs about race move in many directions and affect the choice of a therapist as well as the dynamics of therapy. It is manifest in issues of transference and countertransference—that is, how the client comes to feel about the therapist, how the therapist comes to feel about the counselee, and personal experience—i.e., how the therapist feels about self. Attitudes and beliefs in the wider society impact the client-therapist relationship and the counseling process. Therefore, attention must be given to the role of attitudes and beliefs in therapy. Here we limit our focus to the attitudes and beliefs of therapists.

Earlier we saw that the shaman's personal experiences and system of beliefs were crucial to shamanic performances. Likewise, the family therapist's personal experiences and system of beliefs are crucial to therapeutic performance. A therapist's self-agency is expressed in action, attitudes, and beliefs. Therefore, it is important for therapists to heed the adage, "Know thyself."[12]

Caregivers need to grow in self-knowledge and develop their own beliefs, values, and worldviews. A therapist's self-knowledge as expressed in beliefs, values, and worldview will influence his or her capacity to tap spiritual resources of African American families.

If one can be clear about one's own worldview and open it to critical examination, then it can grow and evolve through experience and the dialogue called therapy. My student, for example, was interested in examining his own attitudes and beliefs and opened himself to a new experience. As a result he was in a better position to understand the importance of growing in belief. Therapists may be better able to tap spiritual resources as they help grow, evolve, and enrich their own beliefs.

This returns us to the question, "Do you have to be a believer in any particular religion before you can help a family with their religious beliefs?" Everyone believes in something whether they call their beliefs "religious" or not. "Belief" is just as important as unbelief and disbelief (or doubt). The question is how do we come to believe in something and/or disbelieve in something else? What kinds of experiences underlie different ways of thinking, reflecting, knowing, seeing, and coming to belief, unbelief, or disbelief? These experiences constitute our frame of reference for whatever we take to be ultimately real.

> Convictions are the beliefs that make people what they are. They must therefore be taken very seriously by those who have them. To take anyone seriously we must take their convictions seriously even if we do not ourselves share them. If we regard integrity and a certain degree of consistency as important elements in being a person, we should neither expect nor want other's convictions to be easily changed or lightly given up.[13]

It is important, therefore, to keep an open, inquiring mind and respectful attitude toward the beliefs of others as well as toward our own beliefs. Curiosity and self-questioning may be a way to develop an open, inquiring mind and respectful attitude toward self and other's beliefs.

To remain open to learning from and respectful toward African American religious and spiritual experiences may be a challenge for those who have been conditioned to view such experiences as a major source of pathology. Freudian-oriented psychiatry, for example, has conditioned many practitioners to view religious experience in this way—i.e., religion is an illusion.

Religious belief, faith, and spiritual resources are central to the family's capacity to develop depth of meaning, and to transform themselves and their world. A dark skinned African American woman wrote, "God never sends us night without the break of day . . . . I would never have been able to write this . . . without the nervous breakdown that I experienced. It was a deep, dark, desolate, frustrating, surviving cycle that I experienced psychologically, and almost never recovered."[14] But she did. Her faith in a God who is everywhere, even in her illness, was a resource that was tapped.

A lot of women have experienced what she did. What is distinctively African American about her experience? She has to struggle not only with mental illness, but also with sexism, racism, and color prejudice. In other words, her oppression is guadruple. She must struggle against mental illness as a black woman in a racist and male-dominated society that prefers lighter to darker skin. In addition, white women are unlikely to perceive or analyze their whiteness as a source of black women's oppression in a male-dominated and white-supremacist society. In a similar way, black men are unlikely to analyze their maleness as a source of domination and violence to black women, children, and to themselves. In order for black women to survive as black women, critical reflection on their oppression by white women and men, and by black men must continue to be a part of their survival strategies. Such reflection may provide hope and is central to the transformation of black communities and the mainstream. For the woman in this vignette, the Divine other is the source for meaning and transformation. Her faith in God served as the basis for her recovery. Of course, religion can also support individual or family pathology when it serves to justify violence, is a source of denial or self-deception, or serves as a barrier to change or growth.

On one hand, when caregivers ignore, deemphasize, or trivialize the religious belief systems in black families, they contribute to a process that disempowers such families. When that happens, the work of a caregiver may be identified with a larger process that strips black families of an essential resource that has, historically, been central to black culture and survival. The family's religious belief system is part of the deep river from which black people have drawn inspiration, fashioned survival strategies, and re-created themselves.

The family's religious belief system is expressed through social practices and organizations, such as the church. I emphasize an important way religious beliefs and practices operate by addressing a critical problem facing African American churches and communities today. Here is the problem: Never-married female heads of household are estimated to make up 43 percent of all black families.[15] This represents a challenge to traditional black church teachings, beliefs, and attitudes toward the family and sexuality. Historic black churches tend to be conservative in teaching, belief, and attitude toward the family, sexuality, homosexuality, women's place, and the ordination of women. For example, sex has traditionally been for married couples and especially for the purposes of procreation. The home has been defined as woman's place, except during times of national crisis such as war or personal economic hardship. Therefore, teenage pregnancy and children born out of wedlock are viewed as sinful. As a result, many would-be church members have been ostracized and have left the church. Instances of teenage pregnancy and children born to never-married females are on the increase and help to constitute what some social analysts call a crisis in the black community.[16] Discrimination, school drop-out, low skill levels, unemployment, and absent fathers are interrelated factors at the heart of the crisis issues and help to perpetuate them. "Dad is destiny," according to a special U.S. News report. "More than virtually any other factor, a biological father's presence in the family will determine a child's success and happiness. Rich or poor, white or black, the children of divorced and those born outside marriages struggle through life at a measurable disadvantage."[17] These crisis issues relate to an increase in crimes of violence, imprisonment, and the inability of many young black males and females to support their families. For the most part, the churches have not been prepared to respond to this crisis creatively. Many have responded out of fear or bewilderment and with condemnation. Consequently, a growing number of young families in poverty have not only been alienated from the black church, but are growing up ignorant of its traditions. Such members of the black community are not in a position to pass on the community's black church heritage.

A few black churches have demonstrated progressive leadership and are creatively responding to the plight of families in crisis. They address different levels of these crisis issues through marriage preparation counseling, parenting curriculum, programs aimed at fatherhood, sponsorship of job training programs, day care, etc. Many black church programs are not well known. The Goodwill Baptist Church of Seattle, for example, sponsors an unwed single black mothers program called the Ardell Mitchell Home. The Mount Zion Baptist church of Seattle has sponsored a day care educational program for many years. Other progressively led churches have developed programs with grants and foundation monies that augment their own resources. Lincoln and Mamiya identified such programs in their study on the black church:

> Conceived by a lay woman, Michele Bowen-Spencer, the Church Connection Project trains volunteer church members to work with the youth of their church. Seminars on controversial topics like the AIDS crisis or sexually transmitted diseases are held. The Bethel A.M.E. Church in Baltimore has also devised Teen PEP (Pregnancy Education Program), which not only attempts to help teenage mothers, but also attempts to involve and educate the young fathers about their responsibilities.[18]

These are examples of churches responding in a crisis situation and fulfilling their historic role as self-help and "natural grass roots community organizations."[19]

Pastor Dr. Wallace Charles Smith provides another illustration of how the black church has addressed this difficult issue of being female and a never-married young parent. We will also see that the family's religious belief system plays an important role.

Miss Elvia Smith is a church member and a never-married, single parent who raised her four sons. "She rarely, if ever received any support from their father."[20] She provided her sons with the nurture and secure base they needed to grow with the help of her church family. "The boys have all grown to be respectable young men. Two of them have completed college, and the others are preparing for college."[21] The church community helped to sustain Elvia Smith's faith by providing spiritual support as she struggled through difficult times to raise her sons. It did this through reaching out during times of stress, uncertainty, and suffering, through its preaching ministry, prayer and participation in songs of hope. During times of uncertainty, these spiritual resources inspired her to look forward to a brighter day.[22] Pastor Smith specifically asked her about the church community as a resource in her relationship with her children. "The church was family. Through these trying times she was rarely condemned by church members, although her first son was born in the fifties when people were not nearly as understanding about such matters as they are today."[23]

In the 1950s, a young woman pregnant out of wedlock was considered bad, weak, lose, impure, immoral, flawed. By comparison, little was done or said about the male responsible for the pregnancy. The young woman carried the burden for the sexual act. A sense of shame and guilt surrounded her and frequently a forced or shotgun marriage was the way to balance a perceived wrong. Sometimes, the young woman was shamed and driven from the church. The pain and suffering from this was, at times, unbearable.

Fortunately, Elvia Smith had a different experience. Belief in God and participation in the spiritual life of her church proved to be the deep river from which she drew during times of crisis. The men in the church acted as role models for her children, and the former pastor, senior deacons, and trustees provided significant spiritual and family support.[24] A religious belief system that emphasizes spiritual values such as agape love, scripture reading and meditation, private and public prayer, song, and nurturing relationships would appear trivial in a secular society that is driven by greed and selfishness, and that measures human worth in monetary terms. Religious values are among the resources that empowered Elvia Smith and enable thousands of other black people like her to transcend their oppressive circumstances.

Elvia Smith's situation may seem mild when compared with other young unwed or single black mothers without the support of the church. Louise Little, the mother of Malcolm X, was put in the position of having to raise her eight children alone when her husband was murdered by white men. She had to find work and to feed and support her family single-handedly. She did so as she was harassed by employers and the state welfare people. Malcolm's mother was a deeply spiritual woman and often had visions. For example, she had a vision of her husband's demise. She was a Seventh-day Adventist, but did not live in a black community, nor was she involved in a black church in the way Elvia Smith was. She was eventually rendered helpless by the forces of racism that surrounded her. Referring to his mother's situation, Malcolm said, "I have no mercy or compassion in me for a society that will crush people, and then penalize them for not being able to stand up under the weight."[25] What was operating in the society and among the welfare workers and others that so thoroughly blocked their compassion and sense of justice?

The way black people express their experience with God may at times appear glib, weak, or unconvincing. Louise Little's faith, religious values, and practices were sources of support as she raised her children. But they alone were not sufficient to combat the collective forces of oppression that surrounded her. She needed the active and caring support of a black community and church.

More frequently than not, there is, among African Americans, reference to the God of justice that includes care for the whole society. Theirs is a belief in a divine, loving presence that binds all life together. Martin Luther King Jr. stated it: we "are caught in an inescapable network of mutuality, tied in a single garment of destiny."[26] This belief in divine love undergirds ideas of justice, the interrelated structure of reality, and social transformation. Holding to this belief is understandable in the light of Elvia Smith's experience, but more difficult to accept in the light of Louise Little's experience. Why not outright condemn a society that continues to crush people, and then penalize them for not being able to stand up under the weight? Why is it that many African Americans continue to embrace a holistic vision in a society that once consigned them to permanent servitude, continues to exclude them, and views them as inferior? Many African Americans are ambivalent toward American society. But most recognize that in times of greatest difficulty their collective faith has inspired, sustained, and helped to deliver them and others. It has helped to prevent "an entire race of people from breaking under the yoke of relentless oppression."[27]

Therapists, then are challenged to continually examine their beliefs, and work for the transformation of the social mainstream in which they and their counselees live, move, and have their being. They can do this by helping counselees to make connections between the troubles in their private and family experiences and oppressive practices in the wider society. A strong tendency among many African Americans is to blame themselves when things go wrong, whether they are culpable or not—e.g., "I should have been smarter," "My skin should have been lighter." Many of the problems that affect them, however, stem from the operation of the economy and the labor market, and from racism and discrimination in the wider society. If awareness of the subtle ways racism and discrimination operate in the mainstream remains low, then therapists' own values and practices will uncritically reflect, legitimate, and help to reproduce these forces of oppression. Therapists who work with black families must go further and tap the spiritual resources that have inspired hope in turbulent and uncertain times. The tapping of spiritual resources enables people to continue the struggle for transformation of the mainstream in which their lives unfold.

I worked with a woman who was given major leadership responsibilities in her religious organization, which she identified as her extended church family. She frequently felt criticized and unsupported by the women in her organization, and put down by the clergymen in authority. For example, she lives in an area where Islam is growing. Her own research and reading suggested to her that Christians need to learn more about Islam as a way to better understand Christianity and Muslims. When she brought up this idea at a denominational business-planning meeting, she was reprimanded and told "that has nothing to do with us." She felt ashamed for having mentioned the idea. There were times she felt no support at all. She blamed herself for what went wrong—i.e., "I should not let these things bother me, I must be weak, my faith must not be strong enough. And here I am telling others to be strong. I must be a hypocrite." She was frequently exhausted and depressed. I focused on her hurt and anger and suggested that perhaps she had been wronged and let down in a big way by those who gave her major leadership responsibilities, but failed to provide support. At first it was hard for her to accept this. She was a preacher's kid and the oldest of two children in her family of origin. Growing up in a minister's family, she was made to feel responsible for setting an example for all of the other children in the congregation. When things went wrong, she was frequently blamed. Hence, she learned early in life to accept responsibility or blame for whatever happened. I asked her to keep a journal detailing what happened every time she led a meeting and to include descriptions of even the slightest show of support. At first she was too depressed to do this. The only relief she could find was in her prayer life, in scripture reading, and in singing. I asked her to describe in her journal how she felt God's support. Because of her religious beliefs, we incorporated elements of these in her therapy. Meditation and prayer, singing, and reflection on scripture reading became avenues through which she could express her anger and joy. Eventually, she became critical of her adversaries, and began to see them as people who were sometimes strong and sometimes weak. She found names for the sexism in her religious group, found strength to speak out against it, and devised strategies for coping. She remained hopeful that her church family could make positive changes. Her family's religious belief system is part of the deep river from which she drew inspiration and fashioned survival strategies.

The ever present challenge for the caregivers is to enable family members to develop a critical perspective by making new connections between their sense of self-agency, beliefs, spirit or life-force, the family's dilemmas, and the workings of the wider social system. Then they can better identify the resources for change or improvement. This may be called reflexive thinking. It is like standing on the riverbank of experience in order to see the shape of the moving river and what it carries. Caregivers can help tap spiritual resources by encouraging the development of this reflexive capacity within African American family members.

Therapy as a Context for Change

The shaman's preparation involved knowledge of context, of the available resources and how to mobilize them for curative or destructive purposes. As the shaman grew in experience, the shaman's repertoire grew in the creative use of context. The same challenge of effective use of context faces today's caregivers-in-training. Caregivers work with multiple levels of context. As members of a complex society, we occupy multiple roles and contribute to multiple levels of meaning simultaneously.

Ideally, family therapy is a healing relationship and a commitment among family members to stop, look, and listen; to come to a decision to change dysfunctional or destructive behaviors; and to grow as moral beings. Therapy can help tap spiritual resources when it serves the above purposes. Its aim is to restore a sense of family care and empathy, to increase a sense of self-responsibility and capacity to invest in relationships of mutual trust and care, respect, and support. But this is a challenge for the therapist because each family is different and has been shaped by its own way of responding to life experiences. Even though families may be shaped by a common language and culture, which they in turn influence and reshape, each family creates its own special style of relating, strategies for coping, and beliefs. Each family has to work out how it will deal with the "petty details" of day-to-day living. These petty details are the droplets of experience, the resources from which the family creates meaning. And these resources are the experiences to be tapped for spiritual growth.

In this light, families have a lot of resources that are not often recognized as such. We can learn to recognize resources from the statements and strategies family members employ in their day-to-day living, whether they use religious language or not.

One day, a young single black woman called and asked if I would help her cope with the new family she had just taken on. I shall call her Mary. Mary was 22, and she had just won court custody of her three younger siblings, whom I shall call Frank (age 7), Susan (age 10), and Robert (age 11). Mary wanted a black male therapist to serve as a role model for her siblings, especially the boys. They had two sessions with a white therapist, felt uncomfortable, and decided not to continue. Mary was explicit in her initial phone call when she said she was looking for a black male therapist.

Mary left home at age 15. Both of her parents had become addicted to drugs and alcohol. They were in and out of various rehabilitation programs, jail, and prison. The mother had lost custody of the children and they were now in the father's custody. Mary described her growing-up years as chaotic. She left home to be on her own as soon as she was able. She finished high school and was employed as a clerk in a supermarket. Now, at age 22, she decided to adopt her three siblings when the court was in the process of taking them from their father and placing them in foster care. Mary went to court and asked for custody. It was granted. Mary wanted to provide a home, a stable environment, and discipline for her siblings. She also had professional aspirations. She expressed that some day she would like to return to school and become a lawyer.

Mary was a resource that, perhaps, few would recognize as such. Fortunately, the court did. In today's competitive world, it is rare that a young single person, with professional ambitions and trying to make her own way, would step forward and volunteer to become the primary caretaker for three preteens. From the perspective of the wider culture, the typical single 22-year-old today has left or is in the process of leaving home, rather than volunteering to take on parental responsibility. Mary's decision, as an older sibling, is best understood in the context of African American culture and family values. It is common practice that an older sibling will stand in the parental role when the parents are no longer able to do so.

Mary found her new undertaking to be overwhelming at times. At first she appeared depressed. With the exception of Robert, the younger siblings would constantly test her limits. Robert would test limits in other ways. When she would assert herself, they, especially Susan, would often say, "I don't have to mind you, you ain't my mamma!" Robert was resourceful in that he would find something to play with, or draw or read during the sessions. Mary referred to him as "very intelligent for his years." He was clever, and yet Mary was concerned about his lying and attempts to shortchange her whenever she would send him to the store. There was a lot of competition or infighting among the younger siblings. It was Robert's attempts at deceit, and the constant fighting between Susan and Frank, and their challenge to Mary's authority that led her to call for an appointment. I asked Mary what she was most concerned about. It was Susan's behavior. Susan would not come home from school as expected, and was hanging out with kids who got into trouble with the law. When Mary confronted Susan concerning her whereabouts, Susan would lie. Mary feared Susan's potential early sexual involvement with boys. I wondered how to reframe as positive and resourceful the sibling rivalry and Mary's choice to become the primary caretaker. If families have a lot of resources that are not recognized, then how can their competitive interactions and attempts at deception be turned around and viewed as resourceful?

As the second session with the family began, Frank got into a heated argument and negative name-calling with Susan. They were arguing and threatening over the use of one black crayon (of which there were several). Frank at the time had the crayon and Susan was trying to wrestle it away from him. Robert watched from a distance, but had busied himself with drawing. Mary was quick to point out that this is the way it is at home all the time. She was tired of it and ordered Frank and Susan to stop. They did and sat on the floor on opposite sides of Mary. I agreed with Mary that it was important to stop the name-calling and threats, and that it was good that Robert stayed out of it. I then suggested that maybe there was another way to think about the use of that one crayon. I asked Frank and Susan if they would be willing to try something new. They showed interest and said yes. I asked Susan if she would be willing to try to ask Frank if she could use the crayon, in the nicest way she could think of. She said, "It ain't going to happen. He won't give it to me." I asked if she would try, and suggested that Frank just might surprise us. She doubted it. I asked again if she would be willing to try to ask in the nicest way she could think of. I repeated this several times. Eventually, she did. Frank immediately gave her the crayon. I thought it important to congratulate and praise both Susan and Frank for doing something that no one thought would happen. I told them how proud I felt for both of them. I congratulated Robert for staying out of the competition and for allowing his younger siblings to work it out among themselves. I told Mary that I could appreciate how discouraging this must be when it happens all the time. Mary wondered, "How long will this last?" I told her I did not know, but that we would work on trying to change things.

Perhaps the arguing over a crayon and its temporary resolution seemed like a minor occurrence, just a drop in the bucket. But I saw their willingness to cooperate as a resource, something to build on. As a result, I found many opportunities to use competition in the family as an occasion to create cooperation. At the end of the first session, I formed a circle with the family. I remembered a statement Mary made when reprimanding Frank and Susan: "We are trying to become a family and learn to work together, because we are all we've got." I thought that the idea of a closing circle might help to reinforce Mary's sense of family by creating a family circle that included me as an outsider. At the end of the second session, when it looked as if we were not going to close in a circle, Susan spoke up: "Aren't we going to have a circle today?" I asked if she would lead us in a closing circle. She did. In the following session, family members initiated the closing circle when they stood and stretched out their hands to one another and to me. In this process resources for cooperation in the family were uncovered.

I saw the family for about five session. At our last session, Mary said they were feeling a lot happier and that she was feeling a lot more confident. A year after they had terminated, Mary wrote indicating that they worked for a while with a black female therapist. They faced a few storms but weathered them and were cooperating much better. She had quit her job, was on scholarship and enrolled in a paralegal course at a nearby college. The children were doing well in school and were involved in community programs such as Scouting and the YWCA, as well as church activities.

The ways African American families respond to their environment can become sources of inspiration and correction to the way people in the field of family therapy conceptualize family. Caregivers, then, need to become aware of the kinds of questions for exploration their training programs encourage or discourage. One has to think of the family not only in terms of the ways it organizes and responds to itself, but also in terms of its cultural and spiritual resources and adaptive responses to the workings of the wider society.

There are several interrelated contexts and different levels of meaning involved in this newly formed family. They include (1) the wider context and values of United States society; (2) African American history and experience with discrimination and racism; (3) the mediating institutions that directly affect their lives, such as the courts, welfare, education, employment; (4) African American culture, family values, religion, meaning and symbol; (5) mental health, which includes the context of therapy; (6) the inexperience and youthfulness of this family; (7) the emotional level that includes the family's recent losses, gains, and new adjustments.

Which level served as the context for interpreting the competition and attempts to deceive among the children? Which level of activity is considered the higher level and which the subordinate? How does one decide? Some levels are considered more important than others for resolving the problem at hand. Therefore, the more important, or higher, level is taken to be the context that gives meaning to the exchanges between family members.[28]

Caregivers need to know how this discussion about "levels" is relevant to work with African American families and to tapping spiritual resources. Religious language, beliefs, and spiritual experiences are often fraught with multiple levels of meaning. When presented with a dilemma, such as family abuse and attempts to justify it by quoting Scripture, as in the case of the man who came to therapy with his Bible, there are moral, physical, emotional, personal, spiritual, family, and societal dimensions to it. How does the caregiver or pastor decide which is the most important level to address? What concerns or norms guide the caregiver's decisions? Where the caregiver chooses to focus is inevitably a legal and always a moral choice.

When the context for therapy is considered, it is usually viewed in a limited way, as taking place only in the caregiver's office. The therapeutic context has been viewed apart from forces on the international horizon that are shaping world economic systems and contributing to political upheaval, starvation, large-scale dislocation, and demographic change. In turn, these changes impact nations and local social conditions. They generate conditions and create traumas that bring people to seek help. Large-scale changes place stress on a declining labor market, increase class and ethnic divisions in local communities, and give rise to new levels of violence and personal traumas. Contexts must be viewed in relationship to broad historical, social, and economic forces, and class and power relations, which have an immediate effect on the everyday lives of people. Hence, the training of caregivers is challenged on several levels simultaneously.

Which level(s) serves as the primary context for our assessment and interpretation? Should late-twentieth-century caregivers in training programs be expected to formulate and engage adequate historical, social, and economic analyses as a way to better understand what is happening to the people who turn to them for help? Is it important to understand the dynamic relationship between personal despair, the emergence of multicultural societies, increased social class and ethnic division, and the exploitation of women and children? These issues are always implicated in specific family therapy and pastoral care situations with African Americans. The analysis that will guide the delivery of services and pastoral care in the new millennium that is emerging will require an adequate grasp of the interplay between the big picture (unprecedented changes in the wider historical context), the middle-size picture (the local cultural and institutional framework that mediates between the lone individual and larger pluralistic cultures within societies), and the little picture (the immediate context of everyday life that gives rise to the specific issue with which the therapist and pastor are now dealing). These levels crisscross and overlap in subtle ways. They pose a challenge for secular-oriented caregivers and pastoral caregivers. Traditionally, and in the worldview of managed health care reform as it is, the little picture has been taken as the preferred level for care.

If family therapy is to be a source of healing for African Americans, then caregivers must learn to tap the family's spiritual resources. This ability to "tap" does not come automatically. It requires knowledge, empathy, skill, and wisdom working together. Caregivers can learn to tap spiritual resources by learning when and how to elicit stories of resistance and survival amidst cultural upheaval. They can learn to effectively work with the positives. They can build on family strengths. They can join with the family and try to understand the strategies the family employs, the stories they tell, and the metaphors they use to sustain hope.

How do families learn the difference between what can be changed and what they must learn to endure? Where do they find the strength to do this? Family therapist can learn to use cultural models for helping families to endure socially induced traumas. They can uncover resources and help expand the family's repertoire of coping skills. Caregivers can learn to draw out family members' reflective capacities as a way to develop depth of meaning and increase their sense of agency.

Common Ground For Family Therapists and Pastoral Counselors

Family therapists who adopt a secular orientation may not see that they have anything in common with those who are trained as pastoral theologians. But there may be some common ground. If common ground can be found, then they have a better chance of aiding the tapping of spiritual resources. Secular and religiously oriented caregivers, although working from different premises, can together offer families an expanded way to envision change and build a future with hope. What needs to be tapped is a language and a vision that nurture the human spirit and give people reason to hope.

The quotation that began this chapter provides ground for a common vision that can nurture hope. "In everlasting memory of the anguish of our ancestors. May those who died rest in peace. May those who return find their roots. May humanity never again perpetrate such injustice against humanity. We, the living, vow to uphold this."[29]

The common challenge for therapists-in-training and pastoral counselors is to empower African American families as a whole and each family member in the interest of strengthening and transforming the mainstream. This is a challenge in a society that continues to practice race discrimination and to create conditions that bred hopelessness. African American families are part of a great water system, and branches of the main river of life. The goal is to change the direction of the mainstream, to help people evolve new and just ways of relating to themselves, to others, and to nature. The goal is to help humanize the institutions in which we all participate, and contribute toward society's transformation.

The family's welfare is linked to the welfare of community institutions, and community institutions contribute to the welfare of society. Society, in its turn, is the mainstream that is enriched by the nurture it brings to the material, emotional, bodily, and spiritual needs of families. This view of society and the role of therapy presupposes multiple levels of interaction and various contexts. Family therapists and pastoral caregivers do important work when they attend to detail, bring a critical focus to what people are experiencing and doing in their relations, and empower them to change the behaviors that contribute to human suffering. They can help to create the bond of community within the life of the church, mosque, temple, or synagogue. How? By challenging certain self-defeating beliefs, evaluating and offering the opportunity to change negative images of self and others, and helping people to find constructive ways to express strong emotions.

Family therapists and pastoral caregivers can help guide positive attitudes and actions toward the ecological system that surrounds all of us and on which we depend. Through a process of critical reflection and heightened sense of agency, therapists and pastoral caregivers can do important work when they communicate the idea that redemptive power is carried in everyday human action. This idea about "redemptive power" is known among Christians as belief in divine providence. Divine providence is the belief in God's care and continuing involvement with the world and the whole of creation. The theologian James William McClendon refers to divine providence and human response as "responsive co-creation."[30] That is, God is responsive to people and works with people for good in the world. Mitchell and Lewter, in *Soul Theology: The Heart of American Black Culture,* identify divine providence as "the most essential and inclusive" core belief shared by African Americans.[31] "Many blacks may not have so precise a word for it, and they may not even know that the idea they cling to so naturally is called a doctrine. But in Africa and Afro-America, the most treasured and trusted word about our life here on earth is that God is in charge."[32] This means that God leads in healing the brokenhearted, giving sight to the unseeing, and setting captives free. This is redemptive power carried in everyday human action. This is another way to affirm the presence of the spirit world in daily life.

136

Redemptive power is a resource and becomes a stream within the great river system. It becomes influential within the lives of everyday people, especially when they gather to celebrate life. This redemptive power working *between* and *within* people I call the dimension of depth. The goal, then is to learn to tap it and to bring forth its resources. Developing the capacity for reflexivity within families and helping to increase their sense of agency will enhance the achievement of this goal. The challenge at the heart of this goal is to enable the realization of love and compassion in concrete relationships. This is at the heart of the gospel of Jesus. But when therapeutic concern stops with personalized forms of care, it may become one more strategy that accommodates an individualistic ethos and aids privatized understandings of love, justice, compassion, and the Gospel. A sense of community and relational power is lost. And our power to transform the main river system is diminished.

Caregivers tap spiritual resources by showing that compassion in concrete terms cannot be divorced from justice. It can work "in everlasting memory of the anguish of our ancestors;"[33] then compassion and justice must work together and lead to liberation in family relations. If we are to find our roots, then spiritual resources must be tapped and released. Then a sense of harmony and balance between people may continue to emerge. Pastoral theologians and family therapists are on common ground when they remember the past and care for the whole world of relations, which includes care for the whole realm of nature (the ecological system). These concerns can be at the heart of their systemic thinking. The levels mentioned earlier—the big picture, the medium-size picture, and the little picture—can be held together by a reflexive praxis and sense of agency that continually weave them together. A systemic perspective must move back and forth between these levels of analysis, uniting them in a comprehensive and compassionate vision of human community.

~

8

THE RIVER METAPHOR AND
METAPHORS FROM THE RIVER

*A River ... has so many things to say that it is
hard to know what it says to each of us.*

Norman Maclean, *A River Runs Through It*

*Eventually, all things merge into one, and a river
runs through it. The river was cut by the world's
great flood and runs over rocks from the basement
of time. On some of the rocks are timeless raindrops.
Under the rocks are the words, and some of the
words are theirs.*

From the film *A River Runs Through It*

*[Deep River] ... is perhaps the most universal
in insight, and certainly the most intellectual of all
the spirituals. In a bold stroke it thinks of life in
terms of a river.*

Howard Thurman,
*Deep River and the Negro Spiritual
Speaks of Life and Death*

Introduction

Therapists and pastoral caregivers have noted the importance of metaphor in their work.[1] In this book, I introduced the river as the root metaphor for interpreting African American families within the mainstream of American society. In this final chapter I note the concept of time that permeates this book. Next I explore the river metaphor and weave together the river themes of the previous chapters, and widen and deepen them into a full stream. Then I draw two implications for further research, and provide a summary and conclusion.

Two Concepts of Time

There are two different, yet interrelated concepts of time that run throughout this book. One concept is time understood as the unfolding of the social system in everyday life. It is the mainstream of society as it appears now and where people face the daily realities of discrimination, earn a living, educate and protect themselves from immediate dangers, and comfort and care for one another as best they can. Anthropologists refer to this concept of time as synchronic, a description of things as they appear at any particular moment. Hence, in chapter 5 I described Martha's experience of loss and rejection, and the decision to end her life at a particular point. Her sense of agency and reflexive capacities were constrained by her immediate awareness of events and time. The other concept is diachronic—time understood as historical development and the maturing legacy of a people, of which the individual is part. Here one is aware of the past as influence on and resource for the present and future. A sense of roots, the wisdom and contributions of ancestors, the ways they improvised in the face of oppression can be a source of inspiration and provide direction under present-day conditions of spiritual anguish or despair. Both of these concepts of time (synchronic and diachronic) are important for therapists who attempt to engage the spiritual resources of African Americans, and important for an understanding of African American spirituality as it evolves. Both terms are used to describe the structure of time and people's relationship to it. "Diachronic" refers to the structure of time as a historical development or as a sequence of events over time. "Synchronic" refers to things emerging together, or time as the structure of things interrelated here and now, the contemporaneity of events.

Therapists are navigators through time and so are family members. Together, they must understand the immediate conditions that will affect the way they navigate, and the wider, historical context of their journey in order to gain their bearings. Without a sense of history one is easily disoriented and can become prey for new fads or vulnerable to currents that can move people toward despair. The whole journey to the sea cannot be seen. What we see is limited by past experiences, our present standpoint, and the anticipated future. And the relationship between what we can see and know is never settled. Therefore faith and trust, courage and risk taking are required for this journey. Navigators must learn to cope with changing conditions and unforeseen events. Although the destination is the sea, there will be different—perhaps radically different—understandings of what they take the sea to mean, different experiences of the common journey to the sea, and a different experience with the Sea.

It will be important for therapists to stay alert to synchronic and diachronic dimensions of time. On the one hand, to work only in the present and in ignorance of the past is to ignore or romanticize the history of white supremacy and colonization. They continue to circumscribe African American presence in the United States. To work in the present without reference to the past is also to ignore the legacy of strength witnessed in courageous African Americans such as Harriet Tubman, Sojourner Truth, Rosa Parks, Fanny Lou Hammer, and many others who have spoken out against white supremacy. Where therapy is practiced in ignorance of the whole American past, it may be impossible to detect how present-day therapeutic practices suppress awareness of African American strengths and promote Eurocentric values as the preferred or superior standard for mental and spiritual well-being. Where the objective of therapy is the adjustment of African Americans within the definitions and power arrangements of the dominant society, then it may be impossible to recognize black history and the history of other colonized groups as providing radically different and alternative views for mental health and social transformation.

140

On the other hand, to work only in the past would ignore the vivid present as the emergence of novelty where individuals take risks, challenge and transform debilitating myths, and develop new ways of seeing and cooperating. The past, then, can be recognized as an indispensable resource. As new events arise in the present, we can reinterpret the past in ways that help us to better understand ourselves as contributing to the transformation of self and society and mature as decision makers together. Metaphor can play a central role in envisioning these possibilities.

Metaphor is the experience or process of seeing one thing (perhaps unfamiliar) in light of something else (perhaps familiar). It is a bridge between the known and unknown, and between time past, present, and future. It is the mental act of carrying a perception, awareness, image, or meaning from one place to another.[2] In that light we might ask, From what strata of experience do metaphors come? They antedate words; they arise from our earliest attachment experience. To use metaphor is to draw from the deepest streams of human experience. We recognize that metaphors are part of our everyday thought, talk, and action. Root metaphors underlie a people's vision of the future and society, guide their actions, and help determine their options.

I selected the river metaphor because it is a familiar theme in African American religious thought. The river metaphor is also complex and multilayered. It provides an imaginative way to talk about spirituality and the rich and varied history of African American experience. It is used as the interpretive frame for developing an ecological view of therapy, a systemic understanding of African American spirituality, development of meaning, reflexivity, and sense of agency in families. I explored this metaphor in light of Norman Maclean's words, "the River has so many things to say."[3]

A river is "a copious natural stream of water flowing in a channel to the sea or a lake."[4] The river's origins are high in the mountains, created by tiny raindrops, snowflakes, or the melting of glacial ice. For instance, the origins of the longest river in Asia, the Yangtze, are in the Kunlun Mountains of Tibet in western China. Rainfall creates trickles, which join other trickles and become runoff streams as the copious natural streams of water cascade down the mountain slope. As streams of water flow downhill, they become brooks and rivulets, and then that copious natural flow we call rivers. Rivers flow into the sea. The Yangtze River, for example, winds its way through 3,400 miles before it enters the East China Sea. Seawater evaporates, forming clouds in the sky. The wind blows the clouds over the land and gives the water back to the land in the form of raindrops and snowflakes.

The river is an ongoing process. It runs through the land and through our lives.[5] Sometimes the river is a menacing presence, especially when it overflows and floods the land. As flood waters, it may leave its old channel and carve a new channel to the sea. At the same time, flood waters can be useful when they bring nutrients to the soil and recharge groundwater levels. From the perspective of the riverbank the river can be described in contrasting and paradoxical terms. It is here and yet gone. It is passing before us, and yet coming. It is a source of life and death. It can be placid at one time and turbulent at another. When the current is swift and turbulent, the rocks that it carries are rolled and slid along the bottom, cutting the riverbed deeper and wider. When the current slows down, or the water becomes placid, then it is possible to see one's reflection in the still water. But it is impossible to catch one's reflection when the water is running. A river, then, has the capacity to mirror, or reflect back, images of the realities that appear before it. On any night of a full moon, one can see the moon reflected in the river. This is the case when the surface of the river is calm. On days of strong winds or during a storm, the surface of the river appears to have lost its capacity to reflect.

The river is a metaphor for time past, time present, and the future. It can enable systemic thinking. Systemic thinking helps us to see connections between the past and present, the problems we face, and the wider contexts of which we are a part. For example, in chapter 1 I argued that African American families are changing, resilient, and adaptive, rather than static. But in order to view the changes, appreciate their resilience, and understand the variety of family forms—such as nuclear, extended, and augmented—one has to comprehend the connections to historical, economic, and political forces operating in the American mainstream. In chapter 2,

I argued that African American families are streams within the great river system of American society. There I raised the crucial question, Where is this large river system headed? The current struggles in which people engage can be viewed as resilient responses to the workings of the mainstream and therefore helping to bring change, or to maintain the status quo.

Present day struggles open or close the door to future possibilities; therefore, metaphors can help us to think about contexts, how they can be transformed, and what appears to maintain stability. The river metaphor is premised on the idea that all of life is evolving, interrelated, and whole. The river metaphor supports the idea that life is an ever flowing stream that is never quite the same. With constant movement and change, the river grows bigger as smaller streams feed into it. Its swift currents carry the stones that grind and broaden and deepen its channel. The word "deep" means "extending far down from the top." It may also mean "extending far back into the past, or far ahead into the future." "Deep" gives dimension to the present. It suggests that any particular manifestation is always surrounded by something that endures and renews.

"Deep River" is the name of one of the best known Negro spirituals. It has served well the African American religious community for centuries. According to Howard Thurman, it is a song of collective self-awareness flowing from the past and "giving rich testimony concerning life and death."[6] The river has functioned as a barrier to freedom, a means of escape, a place of solace, source of food, and the place of baptism. The spirituals in general were watering places for the spirit. "Deep River," in particular, drew analogies from nature. "Deep River, my home is over Jordan." Jordan was that deep river. As a natural river it flows southward from Syria across Israel and into the Dead Sea. But as metaphor or analogy it was the border between life here and eternal life. "My home is over (on the other side of) Jordan." "Deep River," along with other spirituals, was a source of inspiration and courage. Spirituals "provided a windbreak for our forefathers against the brutalities of slavery and the establishing of a ground of hope undimmed by the contradictions which held them in tight embrace."[7]

The concept of river may serve as a root metaphor for family therapy and pastoral care with African American families, and other families as well. It may be an especially potent way to help children to envision ways to bring change in their lives. For example, a colleague reported her therapeutic experience with a 11-year-old African Caribbean child referred to her treatment center. He was having difficulty with reading and writing. His seemingly uncontrollable outbursts of anger in the class room were not tolerated. In addition, he would put himself in front of the school bullies and get hurt.

One day in a therapy session, he talked about someone putting bad stuff in a river that flowed toward a city. If the bad stuff reached the city it could destroy its inhabitants. His therapist encouraged him to use a sand tray to recreate his story and do something about it. Using the sand tray, the child created a river and put fallen trees and debris, creating a dam, that blocked the free flow of the river. This forced the river to go around the city. By using the river's own energy, he was able to change its course and avert the danger. He then built a bridge over the river. Both child and therapist took this external creation in the sand tray to represent the inner work that the child was doing to bring change and hope into his life. A time of potential danger was transformed into a time of safety.

A river is made up of little droplets of water. Water itself has fascinating properties. It has no shape, no size, color, or smell. Water conforms to the container into which it is poured. Humor and play are like drops of water in the life of the family. Humor, for example, can be used to add more humor to an already humorous situation, or it can help lighten a serious situation. It is important for family members to develop their capacity for humor and playfulness. Playfulness, like humor, may arise spontaneously. Family members may take on a variety of roles during times of play. For example, a parent may play the part of a horse and let the children ride on his or her back. A child may fall and bruise a knee. The attending parent may use humor or be appropriately playful in order to calm the frightened child while attending to the bruised knee. The size and shape that humor or play takes is only limited by the circumstance, available resources, and family members' imagination.

A river is a source of recreation and may be a reminder that family play, small and random acts of kindness are like drops of water. When water drops join a river, you can dive into it, bathe, kick, splash, swim, fish, go boating and water skiing. Drops of water renew the river, and small acts of kindness or play create opportunities to renew family relationships. Recreation, for example, represents a time of discovery because it serves as a break from the routine and demands of the workaday world. We saw the important role of play in the illustration above, when a child was encouraged to use a sand tray. He imagined a situation of impending danger over which he thought he had little or no control. He was encouraged by his therapist to re-create the dangerous situation and work it out through play. His playful acts were like the droplets of water that helped to make a difference. Small acts, such as play or humor are like the droplets of water that alter the diachronic structure of social experience and may lead to significant social change. Recreation can lead to new ways of seeing and new patterns of behavior. In this way, time is renewed through droplets of experience.

Sometimes the river freezes. This is a reminder that there are times when family members feel stuck—as if frozen and unable to change an undesirable pattern. The experience of being stuck in an old pattern may signal a crisis—a dangerous opportunity. On the one hand, to break with an old pattern means to give up the familiar. It may entail the painful tasks of ending a relationship or leaving the security of a job. On the other hand, awareness of being stuck in an old pattern may signal a willingness to take risks and experiment with new ways of seeing and acting. The frozen river, then, does not mean that one is immobilized, rather it may represent a different way to think about experience. When the river freezes, you can skate on its surface, or drill a hole through the ice and catch fish below the frozen surface.

Water, whether solid or fluid, can revive life. It can take life. It may also be a source of consolation as well as a place for remembrance. "By the rivers of Babylon, there we sat down and there we wept when we remembered Zion" (Psalm 137:1).

When the river becomes a place for dumping toxic chemical waste, then it can put life at risk. Rivers can be harmed and become the receptacle of acid rain. Through neglect and abuse they can die. But when cared for they restore life and stir the imagination. They sometimes babble and murmur as they churn and turn around the bend. Rivers sometimes divide into many channels or branches. For instance, the Yangtze River divides and takes separate channels as it nears Shanghai on its way to the sea. Families do something similar. Families create their own expressions or sounds as they develop their own symbols, signs, signals, verbal and nonverbal communications. When anger or hatred are allowed to fester and when dysfunctional patterns of communication develop, then family members are at risk. Violence is a frequent outcome. Some families split and when they do family members forge separate paths. This was the case with Martha in her first marriage when her husband abandoned her and their children. Martha and her estranged husband traveled separate paths.

The Nile is another example of a river that splits or divides. It is the longest river in Africa and in the world. It branches into two major channels as it approaches the Mediterranean Sea. A river branch may join another river as a flowing stream or tributary. It cuts through snow-capped mountains, creates waterfalls, leaves cliffs, and forms a lake. Over thousands or millions of years, the river carves a canyon or a deep V-shaped valley. Its rushing waters smooth the stones that rest in its bed. It carves out a niche as it winds its way to the sea. The great Colorado River with its origins in the Rocky Mountains is such a river. It flows southwest, cutting deep gorges on its way to the Gulf of California in Mexico. Its great achievement over billions of years is the Grand Canyon.

A river changes over time. As a fluid structure, the river is never the same. You can never step into the same water twice. It brings about new possibilities and it carries things away. The river is shallow at one point, and deep at another. Howard Thurman described the Mississippi River:

> The Mississippi River . . . rises in the northern part of the United
> States, fed by perpetual snows; at its source it is unpretentious,
> simple. It increases in momentum, in depth, in breadth, in turbu-

lence as it makes its journey down the broad expanse of America, until at last it empties itself into the Gulf of Mexico, which, in a sense, is the triumph of its own achievement![8]

The river's depth or shallowness depends on the riverbed, the season, and the tributaries that feed into it. It depends on change (variability) to remain viable. It knows how to go around obstacles and forge new paths. The river has depth and it has a surface, but depending on the riverbed, you cannot always tell how deep it is when standing on its bank. You may skip a rock across its surface. The rock disappears and reappears several times before it disappears for good beneath the surface. As soon as you touch the river's surface or stick your toe into it, you keep going down until you hit something that is called bottom. The river leads you to its depths and it is never what it seems to be. This description of the river reminds me of the purposes set forth in chapter 4, where I focused on the role of questions in therapy. Awareness of the role of questions is important in work with African Americans. The kinds of questions raised or not raised set the tone for what can be talked about and what cannot. Questions can be used in a variety of ways. One way is to use questions and the therapist's empathic grasp of what is going on, and spiritual resources to achieve depth. Some questions and responses may appear to be superficial and merely skip across the surface of things, while other questions may lead to deeper empathy, trust, and exploration.

I do not attribute self-consciousness to a river, but it has force. Whenever there is a block in the river's path, the river is able to forge its way around the block, thereby creating a new path as it continues on its way. It may be said that the currents of the river can move things along and in predictable ways. Hence, we may talk about upstream and downstream. The river, following the laws of gravity, flows down. But sometimes, the river runs upstream in what is called a tidal bore. "Tidal bores form on rivers and estuaries near a coast where there is a large tidal range and the incoming tide is confined to a narrow channel. They consist of a surge of water moving swiftly upstream headed by a wave or series of waves. Such bores are quite common."[9] Examples would be the Mascaret River or the Seine, in France; the Severn in England; or the Petitcodiac River, which empties into the Bay of Fundy in New Brunswick.[10] In chapter 2 I raised the question of the direction of the mainstream: where is it headed? Are we moving upstream or downstream? What oceanic forces are moving the society? Questions about the preferred direction of American society are answered in different ways by Negro historians and by black historians. Each view holds different implications for therapeutic activity and goals. Is the goal of therapy to adjust African Americans within the mainstream or are there other goals? The direction in which we are moving, whether upstream or downstream, will be influenced by our perception of time, sense of urgency and agency.

Research Implications

There are two implications for further research that I draw from this use of the river metaphor. They are ethical implications and global uses of the river metaphor.

Ethical Implications

I have argued that we live by metaphor, and the shape of our world depends on our use of metaphor. Therefore, our choice of metaphors is an important ethical decision because they guide our thinking and action, and provide us with a language for selective interpretation of the past, present, and future. Metaphors implicitly provide a blueprint for the future. They give us a map for locating ourselves in the present, and they provide us with a way to order our relationships and think about time.

Since no single metaphor can account for the whole of our experiences, metaphors are limited. They conceal certain aspects of our experiences while revealing other aspects. Reason and imagination are constrained by the metaphors we use. To choose a metaphor is an ethical decision because it both aids and hinders what we can see, guides moral reflection, and helps or hinders our sense of agency.

> Metaphor is one of our most important tools for trying to comprehend partially what cannot be comprehended totally: our feelings, aesthetic experiences, moral practices, and spiritual awareness.

148

These endeavors of the imagination are not devoid of rationality;
since they use metaphor, they employ an imaginative rationality.[11]

We note that this "imaginative rationality," though limited, is also complex and richly textured. It unites reason (categorization, entailment, and inference) and imagination (seeing one thing in terms of another).[12] By so doing we discover new ways to navigate and transform understandings of our world and our place in it.

Metaphors from nature can shape our understanding of the social world. For example, we can see the processes of birth, growth, maturing, death, decay, and new life in nature. The river is a metaphor from nature and an ecosystem that supports a variety of life forms. It is bordered by a bank where animals come to live and fish from its waters. It is a complex network of cooperating factors. The river is not only a flow of water, it is riverbed, bank or channel, swift currents, undertow, path, and connection between mountain and sea. It also shows us that we have something in common with the natural environment and all living creatures. Both plant and animal life depend on unpolluted water for health and survival. Therefore, we must recognize our part in the ecosystem as well as in the social system and help to maintain the life-supporting systems of our planet if we want to survive. The well-being of society depends on the health of the natural environment that surrounds and sustains it. This identification with all living things suggest that human beings have a responsibility to care for the natural environment and to keep clean its rivers, lakes, and oceans. This is an integral part of caring for self and others.

Global Implications

Each river is different. Each has its own unique history and journey to the sea. Each carries resources such as minerals, nutrients, soil, and sediment. Each helps to constitute the continuous flow of society. All the great rivers of the world have been given a name, for example, the Nile, the Yangtze, the Ganges, the Thames, the Mississippi, the Colorado, the Han, the Jordan, the Zambezi. Each has a different length, width, shape and size, and level of depth. Each river has a history and changes as it moves from the early to middle and late stages of its journey to the sea. Over time, rivers change their courses. When the river comes close to the sea, it is subject to the sea's tides and seasons, its ebb and flow. Everything that depends on such a river is also affected by the high and low tides. As it nears or entered the sea, it drops its load. The river comes to an end, but not its waters.

Rivers speak to us about death and new life. A colleague recently said:

> Rivers are a very profound symbol in many ways for us Hindus. The ashes of the dead, after we cremate them, are scattered in the holy river so that their souls can be purified and journey to heaven to be reincarnated. Hindus also believe that bathing in the Ganges River absolves all sins.
>
> My father also used to tell me that when our souls were released from their bodies, we must return to the earth what we had borrowed from it. [We must return] the ashes that were our bones, the water in our body which now belongs to the Ganges, and the air to the atmosphere. And the soul continues on in more reincarnations.[13]

The river is a way to interpret life, spiritual renewal, and death in other cultures. For example, the name of the Ganges River *(Ganga Jol)*, means "sacred waters." The Ganges originates in the Himalayas in the north of India and flows southeast through the largest delta in the world, where it empties into the Bay of Bengal. It is used for irrigation and supplies water to several of India's main cities, including Delhi, Agra, Varanasi, and Lucknow. The Hindus call it the sacred waters, holy river, or river of rebirth because it is the place where people from afar gather and bathe to wash away their sins in the hope that they will be reborn into better circumstances in the next world. It is where the ashes of the dead are scattered and carried away.[14] The Ganges accepts the living and the dead, the rich and the poor, the saint and the sinner and all living things. Because it has embraced the deaths of countless people over the centuries it is called "the river of humanity." This deep river carries the sorrows of humankind, of which we are part.[15]

This description of the river may serve as a root metaphor for family therapists and pastoral caregivers who work with African

American and families from other cultures. Each family is different. Each has an environment, a point of origin, a name, a legacy, a way of communicating and changing, a journey and a destination. Each carries resources and creates or fulfills a purpose in the larger scheme of things. The river can be used as a metaphor for life. I view it as an experiential stream that is dynamic, alive, resourceful, and an unfolding process which stirs the imagination. *"The river was cut by the world's great flood and runs over rocks from the basement of time. On some of the rocks are timeless raindrops. Under the rocks are the words, and some of the words are theirs."*[16]

Summary

I summarize my application of this metaphor. Ours is a unique heritage in America—born in slavery, weaned in segregation, striving toward full equality, contributing to the soul of America and imbued with resources to help transform the mainstream, that is, society as a whole and its values. We can draw on the past as a basis for hope while working for wider justice in the present.

African American families have been shaped and moved along by many influences. While African American families are part of a larger unfolding and transhistorical process, each family is in itself an ongoing process. The family is a link between past and future. Its droplets of experience contribute to its unfolding as well as helping to shape the future of America, and larger processes of which all are a part. Its structure is fluid in that it continues to change as it moves throughout the life cycle, as new members are born and mature, and as older members die and join the ancestors. The family is adaptive as it adjusts to changes in its environment and learns to go around obstacles to forge new paths. Each family, as well as each family member, carves out a place, a role, and a way of contributing to the cultural identity and larger whole as life moves on. Sometimes families experience economic abundance, find new ways to expand, and help to lead change. Many experience stability and are able to keep pace with economic change. Increasingly, families headed by single adult females experience hard times. Their capacity to adjust is severely burdened. When they cannot meet the demands for change, poverty deepens, and some disintegrate.

The family is a rich and varied reservoir of experience and experiencing. Family members are like the drops of water that come from the sea and carry the influence of the past—whether family members are aware of it or not. African American families cannot be judged by surface action alone. What you see is not what you get. They have the capacity to be spontaneous and creative, to reflect on experiences, to identify and nurture spiritual values, and to develop spiritual depth. In chapter 5, the nurse assistant was able to achieve depth of meaning with Martha in the context of suffering and a life-threatening illness. Her regular visits reinforced cycles of meaning and brought comfort, inspiration, and hope. I used the term "deep" to indicate that family life is a part of purposes greater than itself. The family's roots are embedded in the rich and varied heritage of African American culture from which its members can draw and evolve. Meaning in life is enriched as family members learn about their cultural and spiritual heritage, and discover themselves in caring relations with others and with nature. Reflexivity, moral discernment, and a sense of agency derive significance from the development of depth of meaning.

The family can cause great harm as well as be the instrument for healing. No one can predict or measure with full accuracy what all of this means. The past exists as a repository of cultural resources; and new resources are created as family members improvise in response to present demands. The family's capacity for resiliency, for critical reflection and renewal or changing directions can be identified, encouraged, and supported. We saw an example of a family's capacity for resiliency in chapter 7 when Mary, the 22-year-old sister, adopted her three younger siblings. The parents had relinquished their responsibilities, but with the assistance of therapists and other helpers the young family members were able to stay together and improvise in response to a family crisis.

Where is the river going? "The goal of the river is the sea. The river is ever on its way to the sea, whose far-off call all waters hear."[17]

The idea that all rivers come from and flow to the sea is analogous to the idea that humankind proceeds from and returns to a primordial oneness that it cannot fully comprehend. Primordial oneness is the idea that life itself emerges from something that is whole, endures, interrelated and evolving, and renews. It is the beginning, the mystical experience of merging or becoming one with God or the Divine Spirit. Where is the river going? It is going toward something that is greater than itself. Human life is moved throughout its journey by a cooperation of forces and by this primordial, underlying process whether individuals are aware of it or not. This is another way of saying that mysticism is at the heart of all experiencing. Mystics feel that they become one with something that is greater than themselves in the same way that a drop of water loses itself when it merges with the sea.[18]

The oneness of humanity differentiates under different historical experiences, and evolves through different cultures and time. It individuates through different genders, ethnic experiences, social conditions, and power arrangements, family and personal experiences, decisions and their consequences. All this is part of the process of our becoming ourselves in an unfolding and interrelated journey.

The use of the principles of development of depth of meaning, reflexivity, and sense of agency in the context of therapeutic work with African American families can help to counter nihilism, which is a sense of despair that grows from the belief that life is without meaning or purpose, and that all efforts to give life meaning are futile. Of course, reflexivity can also be used toward destructive ends. People can reflect on what they have done to others, for example, enslavement. They can reflect on what they have done and then resolve to continue oppressive practices. When Andrew Johnson, the seventeenth president of the United States, made public his position, "This is a country for white men, and by God so long as I am President, it shall be a government for white men," he had thought about it. When the Supreme Court stated its opinion in the case of Dred Scott on March 6, 1857, the Justices had thought about it. Their considered opinion was that African Americans "had no rights which a white man was bound to respect."[19] The problems we face today as a multicultural society, as a people and as individuals, have their roots in this long history of race oppression and cultural domination. The central challenge is the transformation of this tradition, these values, and society as a whole. To give hope to

African Americans, and by extension to all Americans, requires a major shift in direction and national priorities. Hopelessness will continue as long as institutionalized racism, greed, and the exploitation of disinherited people continue to dictate the direction of this so-called democratic society; and as long as we give low priority to the education, health, and welfare of children and give the highest monetary rewards to sports and entertainment figures.

It is true that no one program or strategy can successfully counter the many currents that make for despair in North American society. Yet, therapeutic care in black and African American traditions has always navigated against the odds and in the faith that God works with them to transform society's oppressive practices. African Americans had to keep hope alive amidst the vilest forms of human slavery and suffering. Their spiritual traditions and practices helped them to forge a way when all options seemed closed. That legacy is still alive, but we cannot assume that it will always be there. Care was kept alive because individuals and communities remembered and practiced spiritual traditions of care. When care was able to inspire hope and give direction to people buffeted by centuries of discrimination and waves of despair, it served as counter witness to suffering. In other words, despair can be transformed, and therapeutic efforts must utilize spiritual resources to make a difference.

Reflexivity, sense of agency, and developing depth of meaning are the tools for navigation and they need to be seen as part of a larger process of renewal and transformation, which includes awareness of the whole American past, reaching out to others in the present, reaching inward to tap spiritual resources and, uplifting or empowering people to help themselves *and others*. These need to be among the currents that move us toward the sea. Earlier, I said that when the river is moving swiftly it carries the pebbles and small stones in the current. But the larger stones are rolled along the bottom, cutting the riverbed deeper and wider. The family's difficulties are like the stones. Some are small enough not to be noticed. They are carried in the typical dynamics of day-to-day living. Other difficulties, however, may be like the larger rocks that are rolled along the bottom and act as grinding tools. Viewed pos-

154

itively, they can deepen the family's awareness that significant changes are going on below the surface. Difficulties may help to heighten awareness that family members are decision makers, cocreators, or active participants in an ongoing process of renewal and transformation. Family members may come to view their difficulties as challenges for greater justice. Troubles, then, represent more than dysfunctional relationship patterns, they are also opportunities for assessing how family members are navigating the river and give rise to new opportunities for growth. A sea of trouble may bring out certain unrecognized family strengths and offer an uncommon chance to break disabling patterns, or they may destroy family relations. The meaning of family crisis is that it represents a dangerous opportunity. In the ebb and flow of trouble one may find occasions to include and offer hospitality to those family members who have become strangers, outsiders, or spiritual refugees.

In conclusion, the river is an ongoing process and part of the continuous flow of society. To navigate the river is to become aware of the interplay between the synchronic and diachronic dimensions of time. Awareness of the historical dimension gives perspective to present-day activities; and present-day activities lead inevitably to the symbols and signs we employ to construct meaning in life.

Today's therapists and caregivers are challenged to work in awareness of the symbols and signs that emerge from the most fundamental and enduring values that give coherence and meaning in American culture. If the well-being of society is dependent on the participation of conscious human agents who actively work to transform social institutions and give them new meaning, then caregivers must find a way to tap spiritual resources and help develop meaning in life. The river can serve as a root metaphor for this challenging task. This metaphor is expansive and imaginative enough to include the spiritual life of African Americans and to be used in critical interpretations of the workings of American society, and the role of therapists. Family life, like the ever flowing river, is a repository of all kinds of deeds, and dreams. It is the place for fashioning all kinds of responses that are necessary for the transformation of society and the renewal of personal and family life. Family life is an ecosystem in miniature. It reflects the reciprocal and evolving relationships between an individual and her or his emerging social and natural environment. Ideally, it is a creative place, a place to experience forgiveness and acceptance. Its creativity is embedded in the deeper currents of life, its ebb and flow, and in the routine and ordinary tasks and challenges of everyday life. The unique and extraordinary is the deeper current. It sustains the routine and ordinary tasks of daily life. It is this dimension, the unique and extraordinary, that is implied in everything that exists. To find it implies an ongoing willingness to nurture the search for it. It is "like a current that flows beneath the surface, a current that sets seaward or along the beach while the waves on the surface are breaking upon the shore."[20] Pastoral and family therapists are challenged to increase awareness of the deeper life, and the unique and extraordinary in ordinary time. Reflexivity and a sense of agency are resources that enable awareness of the deeper currents of life. With heightened awareness and courage to act, we may creatively transform the powers that deny human fulfillment.

~

NOTES

Foreword

1. bell hooks, *Yearning: Race, Gender, and Cultural Politics* (Boston: South End Press, 1990), 229.

Introduction

1. Edgar Auerswald, M.D., "Interdisciplinary Versus Ecological Approach," *Family Process* 7, no. 2 (September 1968): 204.

2. See Ross V. Speck and Carolyn Attneave, *Family Networks: A New Approach to Family Problems* (New York: Vintage Books, 1974).

3. Auerswald, "Interdisciplinary Versus Ecological Approach," 313.

4. Rosa Parks and Gregory J. Reed, *Quiet Strength: The Faith, the Hope, and the Heart of a Woman Who Changed a Nation* (Grand Rapids, Mich.: Zondervan Publishing House, 1994), 31.

5. Mark Whitaker, "White and Black Lies," *Newsweek,* November 15, 1993, 54.

6. Cain Hope Felder, ed., *Stony the Road We Trod: African American Biblical Interpretation* (Minneapolis: Fortress Press, 1991), 2.

7. Ellis Cose, "Rage of the Privileged," *Newsweek,* November 15, 1993, 62. Cose quotes from an interview with Dr. Sharon Collins, a sociologist at the University of Illinois at Chicago.

8. Jerry Thornton and Bruce Buursma, "Churches Offer Hope, But Only for the Hopeful," *Chicago Tribune,* December 1, 1985, 34.

9. An important question emerges that we cannot address at this point: Who are the marginalized? They are not a monolith. Rather, they represent a complex and culturally mixed population, different groups with differing needs. They are part of our pluralistic and multicultural society. They are from Protestant, Catholic, Jewish, Muslim, as well as other religious traditions. What, then, are the implications of their growing presence for religious and political institutions and for our democratic society as a whole? How shall the marginalized find voice, be heard, and contribute to the life of society? What changes need to occur in order for black Christian-Muslim cooperation, or for black churches as a collective to address the increasing presence of marginalized people? What are the implications for the way we understand and practice therapy?

10. See Robert Coles, *The Spiritual Life of Children: The Inner Lives of Children* (Boston: Houghton Mifflin Company, 1990).

11. Ibid., xvii.

12. Valerie M. DeMarinis, *Critical Caring: A Feminist Model for Pastoral Psychology* (Louisville, Ky.: Westminster/John Knox Press, 1993), 67–81.

13. Edgar H. Auerswald, "Cognitive Development and Psychopathology in the Urban Environment," in *Children Against School: Education of the Delinquent, Disturbed, Disrupted,* ed. Paul S. Gruabard (Chicago: Jollett, 1969),

14. Ibid.

15. Parks and Reed, *Quiet Strength,* 32.

16. Central to this understanding of depth of meaning, self-reflexivity, and sense of agency is the concept of the relational self, of a self that is constituted, renewed, or deformed by its many relations and activities. This includes memory, the self's purposeful response to it's own activities and to social and historical forces, and relations to time, others, Diety, and the unknown. The self originates in language and continues to emerge in a particular relationship to the Divine Other. It is reflexive in that it comes to self-consciousness, self-control, self-evaluation, and self-esteem through language and relationships. These capacities to use language and self-consciousness are not givens, rather they are the achievements of interactive selves. This idea of the active and relational self implies self-other recognition, dialogue, self-adjustment, and direction through deliberations, discernment of alternatives, decision-making, reflection, and future plans. It also implies the capacity for deceiving others and self-deception. I use the term "self" as synonymous with the concept person or personhood, and use such reflexive terms as myself, yourself, or ourselves. The self has a certain moral status and is a bearer of rights and responsibilities. Because it emerges from language and through close relations, it inherits as well as helps to create a past and present. It anticipates a future, holds values, influences others, as well as undergoes a myriad of influences. Paradoxically, the self is body, mind, and spirit, emotion and intellect, being and becoming, determined and yet somehow free. It is always located or embedded in a community of selves and emerges as a relational self and in a particular relationship to time and place and meaning. At the same time it can imaginatively transcend its spacial-temporal location and envision alternative possibilities and create new meanings. It is capable of developing depth of meaning as the self moves through time, is moved by an inner urgency or sense of time passing, and contributes to an enrichment of life. I develop ideas of the relational self in another work, but here briefly suggest its relationship to this volume. These ideas about the self-in-relations undergird the descriptions of persons in the case vignettes.

17. Thornton and Buursma, "Churches Offer Hope," 34.

18. T. S. Eliot, "The Dry Salvages" (1941), in *Collected Poems 1909–1962* (London: Faber and Faber, 1963), 205.

1. Navigating the American Mainstream

1. Andrew Billingsley, *Climbing Jacob's Ladder: The Enduring Legacy of African-American Families* (New York: Simon & Schuster, 1992).

2. Ibid., 18.

3. Ibid., 35.

4. Ibid., 23.

5. Salvidor Minuchin et al., *Families of the Slums: An Exploration of Their Structure and Treatment* (New York: Basic Books, 1967), 349–79. Also see William Julius Wilson, *The Truly Disadvantaged: The Inner City, the Underclass, and Public Policy* (Chicago: University of Chicago Press, 1987).

6. See Archie Smith Jr., *The Relational Self: Ethics and Therapy in a Black Church Perspective* (Nashville: Abingdon Press, 1982).

2. Navigating Spiritual Impoverishment in the American Mainstream

1. I am indebted to Norman Gottwald for this particular rendering of the river metaphor. See Norman K. Gottwald, *The Hebrew Bible: A Socio-Literary Introduction* (Philadelphia: Fortress Press, 1985), 95.

2. Notes from a private communication with historian Dr. Vincent Harding, who was also a close associate of Dr. Martin Luther King Jr.

3. James H. Cone, *Martin and Malcolm and America: A Dream or a Nightmare?* (Maryknoll, N.Y.: Orbis, 1991), 246.

4. Peter J. Paris, *Black Religious Leaders: Conflict in Unity* (Louisville, Ky.: Westminster/John Knox Press, 1991).

5. Vincent Harding, "Beyond Chaos: Black History and the Search for the New Land," Black Paper no. 2 (Atlanta: Institute of the Black World, August 1970).

6. Carter Godwin Woodson, *The Mis-education of the Negro* (Trenton, N.J.: Africa World Press, 1933), 132.

7. See Gary Younge, "The Gene Genies," *The Guardian,* May 1, 1996, 2–3. The most blatant statements about white superiority and black inferiority are promoted by the so-called "scientific racists." They operate in universities, gain financial support from private foundations, publish in the mainstream press, and have the attention of policy makers.

8. See Pierre Bourdieu, "Cultural Reproduction and Social Reproduction," in *Knowledge, Education and Social Change,* ed. Richard Brown (London: Tavistock Publications, 1973); Alan Sheridan, *Michael Foucault: The Will to Truth* (London: Tavistock Publications, 1980).

9. Sheridan, *Michael Foucault,* 155–56.

10. This documentary was aired on British Television (channel 4) at 8:00 P.M., March 21, 1996.

11. Whitaker, "White and Black Lies," 54.

12. Harding, "Beyond Chaos," 26–27.

13. This statement was made in a private communication with Dr. Vincent Harding on August 10, 1994, while I was teaching summer school at Illif School of Theology in Denver, Colorado.

14. William Julius Wilson, "Cycles of Deprivation and the Underclass Debate," a paper delivered at the ninth annual *Social Service Review, the School of Social Service Administration,* University of Chicago, May 21, 1985.

15. Cornel West, *Race Matters* (Boston: Beacon Press, 1993), 5.

16. Harding, private communication, August 10, 1994.

17. Barbara Lerner, *Therapy in the Ghetto: Political Impotence and Personal Disintegration* (Baltimore: John Hopkins University Press, 1972), 6.

18. Ibid., 4.

19. Ibid.

20. Minuchen et al., *Families of the Slums.*

21. Barbara Ann Bass, Gail Elizabeth Wyatt, Gloria Johnson Powell, *The Afro-American Family: Assessment, Treatment, and Research Issues* (New York: Grune and Stratton, 1982).

22. Ibid., 3.

23. Ibid., 9.
24. Ibid., 203.
25. Ibid.
26. Ibid., 204.
27. Nancy Boyd-Franklin, Black Families in Therapy: A Multisystems Approach (New York: The Guilford Press, 1989).
28. Ibid., 22.
29. Ibid., 89.
30. Romney M. Moseley, *Becoming a Self Before God: Critical Transformations* (Nashville: Abingdon Press, 1991), 103.

3. Not Everyone Feels Welcomed

1. Vincent Harding, *There Is a River: The Black Struggle for Freedom in America* (New York: Vintage Books, 1981), 208. The experience of being a fugitive from slavery and seeking refuge elsewhere is an indelible part of the struggle for black freedom in the Western Hemisphere. From the beginning of their capture and enslavement, Africans struggled to free themselves from white control. During the 1850s and after the Dred Scott Supreme Court decision (1857) many African Americans fled the place of persecution in the southern United States and fled to the North, Canada, Cuba, or elsewhere. To flee the United States was perceived by many to be the only real way to achieve freedom. In another work, I mentioned that my father shared this belief as a young man growing up in Natchez, Mississippi, in the 1920s. He migrated to Mexico, then made plans to leave the United States for Russia. He had given up on America and fled the Deep South forever. He took refuge in Seattle, Washington. Also, black women during the nineteenth century fled when they were no longer welcome in their place of worship. They found refuge elsewhere as did Rebecca Cox Jackson (1795–1871) who fled her A.M.E. church home because she was not allowed to answer her call to preach. She eventually severed her family ties and joined the Shakers. The struggle to be free and to affirm one's full humanity before God and in relations with others was and continues to be central to African American spirituality. See C. Eric Lincoln and Lawrence H. Mamiya, *The Black Church in the African American Experience* (Durham: Duke University Press, 1990), 5, 280.

2. This incident was recorded by Ellen Goodman, a columnist for *The Boston Globe*. Ellen Goodman, "Incredible Story of a Woman from Africa," *The Modesto Bee*, April 7, 1996.

3. Rev. Sandra Robinson, "Women of Color, Religion and Lesbian Identity: African American Lesbians of Faith and Christian Church and Community" (a paper presented to the American Academy of Religion, San Francisco, California, November 21, 1992).

4. See Miriam Therese Winter, Adair Lummis, and Allison Stokes, *Defecting in Place: Women Claiming Responsibility for Their Own Spiritual Lives* (New York: Crossroad, 1994).

5. Anthony Elliot, *Psychoanalytic Theory: An Introduction* (Oxford, England: Blackwell Publishers, 1994), 156.

6. Ibid.

7. Arthur C. Jones, *Wade in the Water: The Wisdom of the Spirituals* (Maryknoll, N.Y.: Orbis Press, 1993), 98.

8. See Daniel L. Smith, *The Religion of the Landless: The Social Context of the Babylonian Exile* (Bloomington, Ind.: Meyer-Stone Books, 1989), chap. 7.

9. Jones, *Wade in the Water*, 63.

10. Smith, *Religion of the Landless*.

11. Theophus H. Smith, *Conjuring Culture: Biblical Formations of Black America* (New York: Oxford University Press, 1994).

12. Ibid.

13. Ibid., 5

14. Ibid.

15. Ibid., 6.

16. Ibid., 5.

17. Jones, *Wade in the Water*, 48.

18. Ibid., 47.

19. Winter, Lummis, and Stokes, *Defecting in Place*.

4. We Carry the Pain and the Hope

1. Tom Andersen, "The Reflecting Team: Dialogue and Meta-Dialogue in Clinical Work," *Family Process* 26 (1987): 415–28; David Campbell, ed., *Applications of Systemic Family Therapy: The Milan Approach, Complementary Frameworks of Theory and Practice,* vol. 3 (London: Grune and Stratton, 1985); David Campbell, Ros Draper, and Clare Huffington, *Second Thoughts on the Theory and Practice of the Milan Approach to Family Therapy* (London: Karnac Books, 1991); Gianfranco Cecchin, "Hypothesizing, Circularity, and Neutrality Revisited: An Invitation to Curiosity," *Family Process* 26 (1987): 405–13; Larry Dyche and Luis H. Zayas, "The Value of Curiosity and Naivete for the Cross-Cultural Psychotherapist," *Family Process,* 34 (1995): 389–99; Ben Furman and Tapani Ahola, "The Return of the Question 'Why': Advantages of Exploring Pre-existing Explanations," *Family Process* 27 (1988): 395–409; Rachel T. Hare-Mustin, "Discourses in the Mirrored Room: A Postmodern Analysis of Therapy," Family Process 33 (1994): 19–35; Thorana S. Nelson, Colette Fleuridas, and David M. Rosenthal, "The Evolution of Circular Questions: Training Family Therapists," *Journal of Marital and Family Therapy* 12 (1986): 113–27; Peggy Penn, "Feed-Forward: Future Questions, Future Maps," *Family Process* 24 (1985): 299–310; Peggy Penn, "Circular Questioning," *Family Process* 21 (1982): 267–80; M. Selvini-Palazzoli et al., "Hypothesizing-Circularity-Neutrality: Three Guidelines for the Conductor of the Session," *Family Process* 19 (1980): 3–12; Karl Tomm, "Interventive Interviewing: Part I, Strategizing as a Fourth Guideline for the Therapist, *Family Process* 26 (1987): 3–13; Karl Tomm, "Interventive Interviewing: Part II, Reflexive Questioning as a Means to Enable Self-Healing," Family Process 26 (1987): 167–83.

2. Penn, "Feed-Forward."

3. Tomm, "Interventive Interviewing: Part II"; Penn, "Circular Questioning"; Cecchin et al., "Hypothesizing, Circularity, and Neutrality Revisited."

4. William Still, *The Underground Railroad: A Record of Facts, Authentic Narratives, Letters, &C., Narrating the Hardships Hair-Breadth Escapes and Death Struggles of the Slaves in Their Efforts for Freedom as Related by Themselves and Others, or Witnessed by the Author* (Chicago: Johnson Publishing Company, 1970), 34.

5. Ibid.

6. Ibid., 104.

7. Ibid., 106.

8. Ibid., 107.

9. Ibid.

10. From an interview with Cornel West, by Teresa Moore, *San Francisco Examiner and Chronicle,* Sunday, March 3, 1996, 3.

11. See Hare-Mustin, "Discourses in the Mirrored Room."

12. These words were attributed to presidential candidate Pat Buchanan. They were recorded in the London newspaper *The Independent,* Thursday, February 22, 1996.

13. George M. Furniss, *The Social Context of Pastoral Care: Defining the Life Situation* (Louisville, Ky.: Westminster/John Knox Press, 1994).

14. Ruth Erskine, "Therapy Teams," *Context: A News Magazine of Family Therapy* 20 (autumn 1994): 30.

15. See Suman Fernando, *Race and Culture in Psychiatry* (London: Croom Helm, 1988); Jones, *Wade in the Water.*

16. See Vernon Cronen, K. Johnson, and J. Lannerman "Paradoxes, Double Binds, and Reflexive Loops: An Alternative Theoretical Perspective." *Family Process* 20 (1982): 91<->112.

17. Adelbert H. Jenkins, "Attending to Self-Activity in the Afro-American Client," *Psychotherapy* 22 (summer 1985): 338.

18. Ibid., 337.

5. She Drew from Her Depths in Time

1. This case was originally presented by the author in "Black Liberation and Process Theologies: Implications for the Care of Black Families," *Journal of Process Thought,* spring 1988.

2. James Wm. McClendon Jr., *Systemic Theology: Ethics* (Nashville: Abingdon Press, 1986), 81.

3. Bernard M. Loomer, "Christian Faith and Process Philosophy," in *Process Philosophy and Christian Thought,* ed. Delwin Brown, Ralph E. Jones Jr., and Gene Reeves (Indianapolis: Bobbs-Merrill Educational Publishing, 1971), 98.

4. The problem of crossing boundaries inappropriately is recognized with increasing alarm and disastrous consequences, especially with respect to clergy sexual misconduct. Such violation of boundaries is never appropriate. See Marie M. Fortune, *Is Nothing Sacred? When Sex Invades the Pastoral Relationship* (New York: Harper and Row, 1989). There is yet another way in which boundaries may be crossed inappropriately. Edward P. Wimberly identified it: "There is a real danger in assuming [the parenting function when it] encourages . . . dependency [and becomes] a real source of ego gratification for the pastor." Edward P.

Wimberly, *Pastoral Care in the Black Church* (Nashville: Abingdon, 1979), 41. At the same time, Wimberly sees a positive function of crossing certain boundaries when it serves to empower persons in need. See also "Bureaucratic Structure and Personality," in Social Theory and Social Structure, ed. Robert K. Merton (New York: The Free Press, 1968), chap. 2, 249–78; Elizabeth Carter, "Supervisory Discussion in the Presence of the Family," in Family Therapy Supervision: Recent Developments in Practice, ed. Rosemary Whiffen and John Byng-Hall (New York: Grune and Stratton, 1982), 69–79; Elaine Pinderhughes, "Afro-American Families and the Victim System," in *Ethnicity and Family Therapy,* ed. Monica McGoldrick, John K. Pearce, and Joseph Giordano (New York: The Guilford Press, 1982), 108–22.

5. bell hooks, *Yearning: Race, Gender, and Cultural Politics* (Boston: South End Press, 1990), 31.

6. Albert J. Raboteau, *A Fire in the Bones: Reflections on African-American Religious History* (Boston: Beacon Press, 1995), 155.

7. Jamie Phelps, "Black Spirituality," in *Spiritual Traditions for the Contemporary Church,* ed. Robin Maas and Gabriel O' Donnel (Nashville: Abingdon Press, 1990), 342.

8. Adelbert H. Jenkins, "Attending to Self-Activity in the Afro- American Client," *Psychotherapy* 22, no. 2 (summer 1985).

9. See Nancy Boyd-Franklin, "Group Therapy for Black Women: A Therapeutic Support Model," *American Journal of Orthopsychiatry* 57, no. 3 (July 1987): 394–401.

10. Linell Cady, "Relational Love: A Feminist Christian Vision," in *Embodied Love,* ed. Paula Cooey, Sharon Farmer, and Mary Ellen Ross (New York: Harper Row, 1987), 141.

6. Therapists' Training to Navigate the Deep River

1. Jerome D. Frank, *Persuasion and Healing: A Comparative Study of Psychotherapy* (New York: Schocken Books, 1974), 55.

2. Neil K. Dawson and Brenda M. McHugh, "Families as Partners," *Pastoral Care in Education* 4, no. 2 (June 1986): 102.

3. Ibid., 103.

4. Niel K. Dawson and Brenda M. McHugh, "Claire Doesn't Talk: Behavioural or Learning Difficulty?" *Gnosis* 12 (1988): 8.

5. Neil K. Dawson and Brenda M. McHugh, "Application of a Family Systems Approach in an Education Unit," *Maladjustment and Therapeutic Education* 4, no. 2 (1986): 49.

6. Ibid., 50.

7. Ibid., 51. Also see, Neil K. Dawson and Brenda M. McHugh, "Parents and Children: Participants in Change," in *The Family and the School: A Joint Systems Approach to Problems with Children,* 2d ed., ed. Elsie Osborne and Emilia Dowling (London: Routledge and Kegan Paul, 1994).

8. J. L. Griffith, "Employing the God-Family Relationship in Therapy with Religious Families," Family Process 25 (1986): 609–18; Gregory Bateson and Mary Catherine Bateson, *Angels Fear: Towards an Epistemology of the Sacred*

(New York: Macmillan Publishing Company, 1987); Boyd-Franklin, "Religion, Spirituality, and the Treatment of Black Families," *Black Families in Therapy;* David Berenson, M.D., "A Systemic View of Spirituality: God and Twelve Step Program as Resources in Family Therapy," in *Journal of Strategic and Systemic Therapies* 9, no. 1 (spring 1990): 59–70; Gregory Bateson, *A Sacred Unity: Further Steps to an Ecology of Mind* (New York: Cornelia and Michael Bessie, 1991); Layne A. Prest and James F. Keller, "Spirituality and Family Therapy: Spiritual Beliefs, Myths and Metaphors," *Journal of Marital and Family Therapy* 19, no. 2 (April 1993): 137–48.

9. Wimberly, *Pastoral Care in the Black Church;* J. C. Wynn, *Family Therapy in Pastoral Ministry* (New York: Harper and Row, 1981); Edwin H. Friedman, *Generation to Generation: Family Process in Church and Synagogue* (New York: The Guilford Press, 1985); J. C. Wynn, *The Family Therapist: What Pastors and Counsellors are Learning from Family Therapists* (New Jersey: Fleming H. Revell Company, 1987); Sue Walrond-Skinner, *Family Matters: The Pastoral Care of Personal Relationships* (London: SPCK, 1988); Edwin H. Friedman, *Friedman's Fables* (New York: The Guilford Press, 1990); Edward P. Wimberly, *African-American Pastoral Care* (Nashville: Abingdon Press, 1991); Larry Kent Graham, *Care of Persons, Care of Worlds: A Psychosystems Approach to Pastoral Care and Counseling* (Nashville: Abingdon Press, 1992).

10. Salvador Minuchin, *Families and Family Therapy* (London: Tavistock Publications, 1974); Fritz B. Simon, Helm Stierlin, Lyman C. Wynne, *The Language of Family Therapy: A Systemic Vocabulary and Sourcebook* (New York: Family Process Press, 1985), 203. Joining, for example, is a technique of Structural Family Therapy to describe the working relationship between caregiver and family members. The caregiver "joins" with the family by respecting family members and their value system, acknowledging and promoting the family's strengths. To "join" is to establish a supportive, caring, and trusting relationship with each family member in order to facilitate change in the family structure. It is not something that is done only at the beginning of therapy, but throughout the therapeutic relationship. I used the principle of joining as an intervention strategy into the wider social system.

11. Wallace Charles Smith, *The Church in the Life of the Black Family* (Valley Forge, Pa.: Judson Press, 1985), 13–14.

7. What Therapists in Training Need to Know

1. Mark B. White and Candyce S. Russell, "The Essential Elements of Supervisory Systems: A Modified Delphi Study," *Journal of Marital and Family Therapy* 21, no. 1 (1995): 33–53.

2. Derald Wing Sue and David Sue, *Counselling the Culturally Different: Theory and Practice,* 2d ed. (New York: John Wiley & Sons, 1990), 166–72.

3. For an excellent review of black spirituality in a single chapter, see Jamie Phelps, "Black Spirituality" in *Spiritual Traditions for the Contemporary Church,* ed. Robin Maas and Gabriel O'Donnell (Nashville: Abingdon Press, 1990), 332–51. An outstanding, innovative, and interdisciplinary book on black spirituality is Smith, *Conjuring Culture.*

4. Ibid., 339.

5. These words were spoken by the pastor, the Reverend Doctor Samuel Berry McKinney, when he introduced the church's first memorial volume of recorded music.

6. See Wimberly, *Pastoral Care in the Black Church;* Carroll M. Felton Jr., *The Care of Souls in the Black Church* (New York: Martin Luther King Fellows Press, 1980); Cheryl T. Gilkes, "The Black Church as a Therapeutic Community: Suggested Areas for Research into the Black Religious Experience," *Journal of the Interdenominational Theological Center* 7, no. 1 (fall 1980): 29–44; Harriette Pipes McAdoo, ed., *Black Families* (Beverly Hills: Sage Publications, 1981); Smith, *The Church in the Life of the Black Family;* Edward Paul Wimberly, *Pastoral Counselling and Spiritual Values: A Black Point of View* (Nashville: Abingdon Press, 1982); Edward Paul Wimberly and Anne Streaty Wimberly, *Liberation and Human Wholeness: The Conversion Experiences of Black People in Slavery and Freedom* (Nashville: Abingdon Press, 1986); Henry H. Mitchell and Nicholas C. Lewter. *Soul Theology* (San Francisco: Harper and Row, 1986); Boyd-Franklin, *Black Families in Therapy;* Edward Paul Wimberly, *Prayer in Pastoral Counselling: Suffering, Healing and Discernment* (Louisville, Ky.: Westminster/John Knox Press, 1990); Wimberly, *African-American Pastoral Care;* M. F. Boyd, "Theological Implications," in *Womanistcare,* vol. 1, ed. Linda H. Hollies (Evanston, Ill.: Garrett-Evangelical Theological Seminary, 1992); Andrew Billingsley, *Climbing Jacob's Ladder: The Enduring Legacy of African-American Families* (New York: Simon and Schuster, 1992).

7. W. E. B. DuBois, *The Souls of Black Folk* (New York: Fawcett World Library, 1961), 141.

8. Gilkes, "The Black Church as a Therapeutic Community," 33.

9. Layne A. Priest and James F. Keller, "Spirituality and Family Therapy: Spiritual Beliefs, Myths, and Metaphors," *Journal of Marital and Family Therapy* 19, no. 2 (1993): 137.

10. Sue and Sue, *Counselling the Culturally Different.*

11. Ibid., 6.

12. Decimus Junius Juvenalis, *Juvenal and Perius,* trans. G. G. Ramsay (Cambridge: Harvard University Press, 1940). There is a reference much older than Juvenal, but I do not know how old.

13. See James Wm. McClendon Jr. and James M. Smith, *Convictions: Defusing Religious Relativism* (Valley Forge, Pa.: Trinity Press International, 1994), 7.

14. Jamie C. Brent and Roderick B. Jackson, *Poetry of Life: How God Works in My Life* (Oakland: GMW Publisher, 1990), 6.

15. U.S. Bureau of the Census, *Statistical Abstract of the United States* (Washington, D.C., 1995), 63.

16. Lincoln and Mamiya, *The Black Church in the African American Experience,* 332.

17. "Honor Thy Children," *U.S. News,* February 27, 1995, 39.

18. Lincoln and Mamiya, *The Black Church in African American Experience,* 340.

19. Ibid., 341.

20. Smith, *The Church in the Life of the Black Family*, 14.

21. Ibid.

22. Ibid., 15.

23. Ibid.

24. Ibid.

25. Malcolm X, *The Autobiography of Malcolm X*, ed. Alex Haley (New York: Grove, 1965), 22.

26. Foreword by Coretta Scott King, in Martin Luther King, *Strength to Love* (Great Britain: Hodder and Stoughton, 1964).

27. Ibid., 15.

28. Vernon E. Cronen, Kenneth M. Johnson, John W. Lannamann, "Paradoxes, Double Binds, and Reflexive Loops: An Alternative Theoretical Perspective," *Family Process* 20 (March 1982): 91–112.

29. The Independent, Sunday, May 5, 1996, 73.

30. James Wm. McClendon Jr., *Systematic Theology: Doctrine* (Nashville: Abingdon Press, 1994), 180.

31. Mitchell and Lewter, *Soul Theology*, 14.

32. Ibid.

33. *The Independent*, Sunday, May 5, 1996.

8. The River Metaphor and Metaphors from the River

1. Wimberly, *African-American Pastoral Care*; Sharon Parks, *The Critical Years* (San Francisco: Harper and Row, 1986); Brita L. Gill-Austern, "The Role of Christian Community in Pastoral Care: Toward the Transformation of Anxiety and the Development of Trust" (Ph.D diss., Graduate Theological Union, Berkeley, 1991); Henri J. M. Nouwen, *Behold the Beauty of the Lord: Praying with Icons* (Notre Dame: Ave Maria Press, 1987); Jo Milgrom, *Handmade Midrash: Visual Theology* (Philadelphia: Jewish Publication Society, 1991); Raymond W. Peterson, "The Collaborative Metaphor Technique: Using Ericksonian (Milton H.) Techniques and Principles in Child, Family, and Youth Care Work," *Journal of Child Care* 3, no. 4 (1988): 11–27; Roger Lowe, "Re-imaging Family Therapy: Choosing the Metaphors We Live By," *Australian and New Zealand Journal of Family Therapy* (Brisbane College of Advanced Education, School of Health and Welfare Studies, Caseldine, Australia) 11, no. 1 (March 1990): 1–9; Raymond Fox, "What Is Meta For?" *Clinical Social Work Journal* 17, no. 3 (fall 1989): 233–44; Barbara Pees, "Strategies for Solving Children's Problems Understood as Behavior Metaphors," *Journal of Strategic and Systemic Therapies* 8, no. 2–3 (summer–fall 1989): 22–25; Layne A. Prest and James F. Keller, "Spirituality and Family Therapy: Spiritual Beliefs, Myths, and Metaphors," *Journal of Marital and Family Therapy* 19, no. 2 (April 1993): 137–48.

2. See Bunny S. Duhl, *From the Inside Out and Other Metaphors: Creative and Integrative Approaches to Training in Systems Thinking* (New York: Brunner/Mazel, 1983), 129.

3. Norman Maclean, *A River Runs Through It and Other Stories* (Chicago: University of Chicago Press, 1976), 104.

4. Joyce M. Hawkins and Robert Allen, *The Oxford Encyclopedic English Dictionary* (Oxford: Clarendon Press, 1991), 1246.

5. A paraphrase from the film *A River Runs Through It* from Richard Friedenberg, *A River Runs Through it: Bringing a Classic to the Screen* (Livington, Mont.: Clark City Press, 1992).

6. Howard Thurman, *Deep River and the Negro Spiritual Speaks of Life and Death* (Richmond, Ind.: Friends United Press, 1975), 12.

7. Ibid., general introduction.

8. Ibid., 67.

9. *The New Encyclopaedia Britannica*, 15th ed., vol. 25 (Chicago: University of Chicago Press, 1987), 138.

10. *The Woman's Journal* reported, "The recent earthquake in California proves much more serious than was at first supposed. . . . A chasm thirty-five miles in length was opened in Luyo County, varying in width from three inches to forty feet. Kern and Owen's rivers turned their courses and ran up stream for several minutes, leaving their beds dry, but afterwords returned with increased violence" (Saturday, April 6, 1872, p. 109).

11. George Lakoff and Mark Johnson, *Metaphors We Live By* (Chicago: University of Chicago Press, 1980), 193.

12. Ibid.

13. A private communication written on June 19, 1996.

14. A Bangladeshi medical doctor pointed out that the Ganges River is also a source of cholera.

15. Shusaku Endo, *Deep River* (New York: New Directions, 1994), 211.

16. Maclean, *A River Runs Through It*.

17. Thurman, *Deep River*, 73.

18. Jostein Gaarder, *Sophie's World* (London: Phoenix House, 1995), 115.

19. Deirdre Mullane, ed., *Crossing the Danger Water: Three Hundred Years of African American Writing* (New York: Anchor Books/Doubleday, 1993), 132.

20. John S. Dunne, *Time and Myth: A Meditation on Storytelling as an Exploration of Life and Death* (Notre Dame: University of Notre Dame Press, 1975), 6.

~

SELECTED BIBLIOGRAPHY

Achebe, Chinua, and C. L. Innes, eds. *Contemporary African Short Stories.* London: Heinemann, 1992.

Ahmad, Bandana. *Black Perspectives in Social Work.* Birmingham, England: Ventura Press, 1990.

Andersen, Tom. "The Reflecting Team: Dialogue and Meta-Dialogue in Clinical Work." *Family Process* 26 (1987): 415–28.

Auerswald, E. H. "Cognitive Development and Psychopathology in the Urban Environment." In *Children Against School: Education of the Delinquent, Disturbed, Disrupted,* edited by Paul S. Gruabard. Chicago: Jollett: 1969.

———. "Epistemological Confusion in Family Therapy and Research." *Family Process* 26 (1987): 317–30.

Baer, Hans A. "Bibliography of Social Science. Literature on Afro-American Religion in the United States." *Review of Religious Research* 29 (1988): 413–30.

Barker, Philip. *Using Metaphors in Psychotherapy.* New York: Brunner/Mazel, 1985.

Barnes, Gill Gorell. "Systems Theory and Family Theory." In *Modern Child Psychiatry,* edited by M. W. Rutter and L. Herzov, 216–29. 2d ed. Oxford: Blackwell Scientific Publications, 1985.

Bass, Barbara Ann, Gail Elizabeth Wyatt, and Gloria Johnson Powell. *The Afro-American Family: Assessment, Treatment, and Research Issues.* New York: Grune and Stratton, 1982.

Bateson, Gregory. *Mind and Nature: A Necessary Unity.* London: Wildwood House, 1979.

———. *A Sacred Unity: Further Steps to an Ecology of Mind.* New York: Cornelia and Michael Bessie, 1991.

Bateson, Gregory, and Mary Catherine Bateson. *Angels Fear: Towards an Epistemology of the Sacred.* New York: Macmillan Publishing Company, 1987.

Berenson, David. "A Systemic View of Spirituality: God and Twelve Step Program as Resource in Family Therapy." *Journal of Strategic and Systemic Therapies* 9 (1990): 59–70.

Berger, John. *Ways of Seeing.* London: British Broadcasting Corporation and Penguin Books, 1985.

Bertoaux, Daniel, ed. *Biography and Society: The Life History Approach in the Social Sciences.* London: Sage Publication, 1981.

Billingsley, Andrew. *Climbing Jacob's Ladder: The Enduring Legacy of African-American Families.* New York: Simon & Schuster, 1992.

The Black Scholar: Journal of Black Studies and Research 17, no. 5 (1986).

Bourdieu, Pierre. *The Logic of Practice.* Cambridge, England: Polity Press, 1990.

———. *Outline of A Theory of Practice.* New York: Cambridge University Press, 1972.

Boyd-Franklin, Nancy, "Group Therapy for Black Women: A Therapeutic Support Model." *American Journal of Orthopsychiatry* 57 (1987): 394–401.
———. *Black Families in Therapy: A Multisystems Approach.* New York: The Guilford Press, 1989.
Brent, Jamie C., and Roderick B. Jackson. *Poetry of Life: How God Works in My Life.* Oakland: GMW Publisher, 1990.
Brown, Donald B., and Myrtle Parnell. "Mental Health Services for the Urban Poor: A Systems Approach." In *The Social and Political Contexts of Family Therapy,* edited by Marsha Pravder Mirkin, 215–35. Boston: Allyn & Bacon, 1990.
Brown, Richard. *Knowledge, Education and Cultural Change.* London Tavistock Publications, 1973.
Cady, Linell. "Relational Love: A Feminist Christian Vision." In *Embodied Love,* edited by Paula Cooey, Sharon Farmer, and Mary Ellen Ross, 135–49. New York: Harper Row, 1987.
Campbell, David, ed. *Applications of Systemic Family Therapy: The Milan Approach, Complementary Frameworks of Theory and Practice.* Vol. 3. London: Grune and Stratton, 1985.
Campbell, David, Ros Draper, and Clare Huffington. *Second Thoughts on the Theory and Practice of the Milan Approach to Family Therapy.* London: Karnac Books, 1991.
Cecchin, Gianfranco. "Hypothesizing, Circularity, and Neutrality Revisited: An Invitation to Curiosity." *Family Process* 26 (1987): 405–13.
Clark, Malcolm. *Perplexity and Knowledge: An Inquiry into the Structure of Questioning.* The Hague: Martinus Nifhoff, 1972.
Coles, Robert. *The Spiritual Life of Children: The Inner Lives of Children.* Boston: Houghton Mifflin Company, 1990.
Cone, James H. Martin and Malcolm and America: *A Dream or a Nighmare?* Maryknoll, N.Y.: Orbis, 1991.
Cooper, J. C. *An Illustrated Encyclopaedia of Traditional Symbols.* London: Thames and Hudson, 1978.
Cronen, Vernon E., Kenneth M. Johnson, and John W. Lannaman. "Paradoxes, Double Binds, and Reflexive Loops: An Alternative Theoretical Perspective." *Family Process* 20 (1982): 91–112.
Daley, Kerry J. *Families and Time: Keeping Pace in a Hurried Culture.* London: Sage Publications, 1996.
DeMarinis, Valerie M. *Critical Caring: A Feminist Model for Pastoral Psychology.* Louisville, Ky.: Westminster/John Knox Press, 1993.
DuBois, W. E. B. *The Souls of Black Folk.* New York: Bantam Books, 1903.
Duhl, Bunny S. *From the Inside Out and Other Metaphors: Creative and Integrative Approaches to Training in Systems Thinking.* New York: Brunner/Mazel, 1983.
Duncan, Dayton. *Miles from Nowhere: In Search of the American Frontier.* New York: Penguin Books, 1994.
Dunne, John S. *Time and Myth: A Meditation on Storytelling as an Exploration of Life and Death.* Notre Dame: University of Notre Dame Press, 1973.

Dwivedi, Kedar N., and Ved P. Varma, eds. *Meeting the Needs of Ethnic Minority Children: A Handbook for Professionals*. London: Jessica Kingsley Publishers, 1996.

Dyche, Larry, and Luis H. Zayas. "The Value of Curiosity and Naivete for the Cross-Cultural Psychotherapist." *Family Process* 34 (1995): 389–99.

Dyson, Michael Eric. *Race Rules: Navigating the Color Line*. New York: Addison-Wesley, 1996.

Falicor, Celia Jaes, "Training to Think Culturally: A Multidimensional Comparative Framework. " *Family Process* 34 (1995): 373–88.

Felder, Cain Hope. *Troubling Biblical Waters: Race, Class and Family*. New York: Orbis Books, 1989.

Felder, Cain Hope, ed. *Stony the Road We Trod: African American Biblical Interpretation*. Minneapolis: Fortress Press, 1991.

Felton, Carroll M., Jr. *The Care of Souls in the Black Church*. New York: Martin Luther King Fellows Press, 1980.

Fernando, Suman. *Mental Health, Race and Culture*. London: McMillan/Mind Publications, 1991.

Fernando, Suman, ed. *Mental Health in a Multi-Ethnic Society: A Multi-Disciplinary Handbook*. London: Routledge, 1995.

Fleuridas, C., T. S. Nelson, and D. M. Rosenthal. "The Evolution of Circular Questions: Training Family Therapists." *Journal of Marital and Family Therapy* 12 (1986): 113–27.

Fox, Raymond. "What Is Meta For?" *Clinical Social Work Journal* 17 (1989): 233–44.

Friedenberg, Richard. *A River Runs Through it: Bringing a Classic to the Screen*. Livington, Mont.: Clark City Press, 1992.

Furman, Ben, and Tapani Ahola. "The Return of the Question 'Why': Advantages of Exploring Pre-existing Explanations." *Family Process* 27 (1988): 395–409.

Furniss, George M. *The Social Context of Pastoral Care: Defining the Life Situation*. Louisville, Ky.: Westminster John Knox Press, 1994.

Gates, Henry Louis, Jr., and Cornel West. *The Future of the Race*. New York: Random House, 1996.

Geertz, Clifford. "The Uses of Diversity." *Michigan Quarterly Review* 25 (1986): 105–23.

Gerger, Kenneth J., and Keith E. Davies, eds. *The Social Construction of the Person*. New York: Springer-Verlag, 1985.

Gilkes, Cheryl Townsend. "The Storm and the Light: Church, Family, Work and Social Crisis in the African-American Experience." In *Family and Religion in Contemporary Society*, edited by Nancy Tatom Ammermon and Wade Clark Roof. New York: Routledge, 1995.

———. "The Black Church as a Therapeutic Community: Suggested Areas for Research into the Black Religious Experience." *Journal of the Interdenominational Theological Center* 8 (1980): 29–44.

Gill-Austern, Brita. *The Role of Christian Community in Pastoral Care: Toward the Transformation of Anxiety and the Development of Trust.* Ph.D. diss., Graduate Theological Union, Berkeley, 1991.

Graham, Larry Kent. *Care of Persons, Care of Worlds: A Psychosystems Approach to Pastoral Care and Counselling.* Nashville: Abingdon Press, 1992.

Griffith, Marvellen S., and Paul R. Coleman. *Family Therapy: An Ecological Perspective.* Greeley, Colo.: Health Psychology Publications, 1988.

Haber, Russell. "Friends in Family Therapy: Use of a Neglected Resource." *Family Process* 26 (1987): 269–81.

Haley, Joy. *Uncommon Therapy: The Psychiatric Techniques of Milton H. Erickson.* New York: W. W. Norton & Company, 1973.

Harding, Vincent. "Beyond Chaos: Black History and the Search for the New Land." *Black Paper* no. 2. Atlanta: Institute of the Black World, August 1970.

———. *Hope and History: When We Must Show the Story of the Movement.* New York: Orbis Books, 1991.

———. *The Other American Revolution.* Los Angeles: University of California Centre for Afro-American Studies, 1980.

———. *There Is a River: The Black Struggle for Freedom in America.* New York: Vintage Books, 1983.

———. "Toward a Darkly Radiant Vision of America's Truth." *Cross Currents* 37 (1987): 1–16.

Hare-Mustin, Rachel T. "Discourses in the Mirrored Room: A Postmodern Analysis of Therapy." *The Family Process* 33 (1994): 19–35.

Hekman, Susan J. *Hermeneutics and the Sociology of Knowledge.* Notre Dame: University of Notre Dame Press, 1986.

Hollies, Linda H., ed. *Womanistcare.* Vol. 1. Evanston, Ill.: Garrett-Evangelical Theological Seminary, 1992.

Holmes, Thomas. "Spirituality in Systemic Practice: An Internal Family Systems Perspective." *Journal of Systemic Therapies* 13 (1994): 26–35.

hooks, bell. *Yearning: Race, Gender and Cultural Politics.* Boston: South End Press, 1990.

hooks, bell, and Cornel West. *Breaking Bread: Insurgent Black Intellectual Life.* Boston: South End Press, 1991.

Hopkins, Dwight N., and George C. L. Cummings, eds. *Cut Loose Your Stammering Tongue: Black Theology in the Slave Narratives.* Maryknoll, N.Y.: Orbis Books, 1992.

Imber-Black, Evan. *Families and Larger Systems: A Family Therapist's Guide Through the Labyrinth.* New York: The Guilford Press, 1988.

———. "Multiple Embedded Systems." In *The Social and Political Contexts of Family Therapy,* edited by Marsha Pravder Mirkin, 3–18. Boston: Allyn & Bacon, 1990.

Jones, Arthur C. *Wade in the Water: The Wisdom of the Spirituals.* New York: Orbis Books, 1993.

Kaufman, Gordon D., *In Face of Mystery: A Constructive Theology.* Cambridge: Harvard University Press, 1993.

Kim, Uichol, and John W. Berry, eds. *Indigenous Psychologies: Research and Experience in Cultural Context.* Newbury Park, Calif.: Sage Publications, 1993.

King, Martin Luther. *Strength to Love.* Great Britain: Hodder and Stoughton, 1964.

Krause, Inga-Britt. "Personhood, Culture and Family Therapy." *Journal of Family Therapy* 17 (1995): 363–72.

Kunnie, Julian. *Models of Black Theology: Issues in Class, Culture and Gender.* Valley Forge, Pa.: Trinity Press International, 1994.

Lakoff, George, and Mark Johnson. *Metaphors We Live By.* Chicago: University of Chicago Press, 1980.

Lawrence-Lightfoot, Sara. *I've Known Rivers: Lives of Loss and Liberation.* New York: Merloyd Lawrence, 1994.

Lerner, Barbara. *Therapy in the Ghetto: Political Impotence and Personal Disintegration.* Baltimore: Johns Hopkins University Press, 1972.

Levi-Strauss, Claude. *Structural Anthropology.* New York: Basic Books, 1963.

Lincoln, C. Eric, and Lawrence H. Mamiya. *The Black Church in the African-American Experience.* Durham: Duke University Press, 1990.

Loomer, Bernard M. "Christian Faith and Process Philosophy." In *Process Philosophy and Christian Thought,* edited by Delwin Brown, Raply E. Jones Jr., and Gene Reeves. Indianapolis: Bobbs-Merrill Educational Publishing, 1971.

Lorde, Audre. *Sister Outsider: Essays and Speeches.* (Freedom: Calif.: The Crossing Press, 1984.

Lovett, Leonard. *Black Holiness—Pentecostalism: Implications for Ethics and Social Transformation.* Ann Arbor, Mich.: University Microfilms International, 1982.

Lowe, Roger. "Re-imaging Family Therapy: Choosing the Metaphors We Live By." *Australian and New Zealand Journal of Family Therapy* (Brisbane College of Advanced Education, School of Health and Welfare Studies, Caseldine, Australia) 11 (1990): 1–9.

Maclean, Norman. *A River Runs Through It and Other Stories.* Chicago: University of Chicago Press, 1976.

MacMurray, John. *Persons in Relation.* Atlantic Highlands, N.J.: Humanities Press International, 1991.

Malcolm X. *The Autobiography of Malcolm X.* London: Hutchinson, Penguin Books, 1965.

Mbiti, John S. *African Religions and Philosophies.* New York: Doubleday, 1970.
———. "African Theology." *Worldview* 16, no. 8 (1973): 33.
———. "An African Views American Black Theology." *Worldview* 17, no. 8 (1979): 41.
———. *Concepts of God in Africa.* New York: Praeger, 1970.

McAdoo, Harriette Pipes, ed. Black Families. Beverly Hills: Sage Publications, 1981.
———. *Family Ethnicity: Strength in Diversity.* Newbury Park Calif.: Sage Publications, 1993.

McClendon, James Wm., Jr. *Systematic Theology: Doctrine.* Vol. 2. Nashville: Abingdon Press, 1994.

McClendon, James Wm., Jr., and James M. Smith. *Convictions: Defusing Religious Relativism.* Valley Forge, Pa.: Trinity Press International, 1994.

McCoy, Charles S. "Introduction." In *The Meaning of Theological Reflection.* Faith Learning Studies: A Series Examining the Academic Disciplines. New York: Faculty Christian Fellowship, 1964.

Mead, George Herbert. *The Philosophy of the Present.* La Salle, Ill.: The Open Court Publishing Company, 1959.

Milgrom, Jo. *Handmade Midrash: Visual Theology.* Philadelphia: Jewish Publication Society, 1991.

Mills, C. Wright. *The Sociolological Imagination.* London: Oxford University Press, 1959.

Minuchen, Salvador, et al. *Families of the Slums: An Exploration of Their Structure and Treatment.* New York: Basic Books, 1967.

Mitchell, Henry H. *Black Belief.* New York: Harper and Row, 1975.

Mitchell, Henry H., and Nicholas C. Lewter. *Soul Theology: The Heart of American Black Culture:* San Francisco: Harper and Row, 1986.

Mossley, Romney M. *Becoming a Self Before God: Critical Transformations.* Nashville: Abingdon Press, 1991.

Mpoto, Jean Mascimba ma, and Daisy Nwrehuku, eds. *Pastoral Care and Counselling in Africa Today.* Frankfurt am Main: Peter Lang, 1991.

Nelson, Thorana S., Colette Fleuridas, and David M. Rosenthal. "The Evolution of Circular Questions: Training Family Therapists." *Journal of Marital and Family Therapy* 12 (1986): 113–27.

Nisbet, Robert A. *Social Change and History.* New York: Oxford University Press, 1969.

Nobles, Wade W. *Africanity and the Black Family: The Development of a Theoretical Model.* Oakland, Calif.: The Institute for the Advanced Study of Black Family Life and Culture, 1985.

————. *African Psychology: Toward Its Reclamation, Reascension, and Revitalization.* Oakland, Calif.: The Institute for the Advanced Study of Black Family Life and Culture, 1986.

Nobles, Wade W., and Lawford L. Goddard. *Understanding the Black Family: A Guide for Scholarship and Research.* Oakland, Calif.: Black Family Institute, 1984.

One Small Step Towards Racial Justice: The Teaching of Anti-racism in Diploma in Social Work Programmes. Improving Social Work Education and Training. Vol. 8. London: Central Council for Education and Training in Social Work, 1991.

Pakman, Marcelo. "Therapy in Contexts of Poverty and Ethnic Dissonance: Constructivism and Social Constructionism as Methodologies for Action." *Journal of Systemic Therapies* 14 (1995): 64–71.

Papp, Peggy, and Evan Imber-Block. "Family Themes: Transmission and Transformation." *Family Process* 35 (1966): 5–20.

Pare, David A. "Culture and Meaning: Expanding the Metaphorical Repertoire of Family Therapy." *Family Process* 35 (1996): 21–42.

Paris, Peter J. *The Spirituality of African Peoples: The Search for a Common Moral Discourse.* Minneapolis: Fortress Press, 1995.

Parks, Rosa, and Gregory J. Reed. *Quiet Strength: The Faith, the Hope, and the Heart of a Woman Who Changed a Nation.* Grand Rapids, Mich.: Zondervan Publishing House, 1994.

Pees, Barbara. "Strategies for Solving Children's Problems Understood as Behavior Metaphors." *Journal of Strategic and Systemic Therapies* 8, no. 2–3 (summer–fall 1989): 22–25.

Penn, Peggy. "Circular Questioning." *Family Process* 21 (1982): 267–80.

———. "Feed-Forward: Future Questions, Future Maps." *Family Process* 24 (1985): 299–310.

Peterson, Raymond W. "The Collaborative Metaphor Technique: Using Ericksonian (Milton H.) Techniques and Principles in Child, Family, and Youth Care Work." *Journal of Child Care* 3 (1988): 11–27.

Phelps, Jamie. "Black Spirituality." In *Spiritual Traditions for the Contemporary Church,* edited by Robin Maas and Gabriel O'Donnell. Nashville: Abingdon Press, 1990.

Pilisuk, Marc, Susan Hillier Parks. *The Healing Web: Social Networks and Human Survival.* Hanover, N.H.: University Press of New England, 1986.

Plath, David W. *Long Engagements: Maturity in Modern Japan.* Stanford: Stanford University Press, 1980.

Prest, Layne A., and James F. Keller. "Spirituality and Family Therapy: Spiritual Beliefs, Myths and Metaphors." *Journal of Marital and Family Therapy* 19 (1993): 137–48.

Pryse, Marjorie, and Hortense J. Spillers, eds. *Conjuring Black Women: Fiction and Literary Tradition.* Bloomington: Indiana University Press, 1985.

Raboteau, Albert J. *A Fire in the Bones: Reflections on African-American Religious History.* Boston: Beacon Press, 1995.

Rosenblatt, Paul C. *Metaphors of Family Systems Theory: Toward New Constructions.* New York: The Guilford Press, 1994.

Ross, Joellyn L. "Working with Patients within Their Religious Contexts: Religion, Spirituality, and the Secular Therapist." *Journal of Systemic Therapies* 13 (1994): 7–15.

Rowan, Carl T. *The Coming Race War in America: A Wake-up Call.* New York: Little, Brown and Company, 1996.

Sampson, Edward E. *Ego at the Threshold: In Search of Man's Freedom.* New York: Delta, 1975.

———. *Justice and the Critique of Pure Psychology.* New York: Plenum Press, 1983.

Scheper-Hughes, N., and C. Sargent. *The Cultural Politics of Childhood.* Berkeley: University of California Press, 1996.

Schutz, Alfred. *Reflections on the Problem of Relevance.* New Haven: Yale University Press, 1970.

Selvini-Palazzoli, M., et al. "Hypothesizing-Circularity-Neutrality: Three Guidelines for the Conductor of the Session." *Family Process* 19 (1980): 3–12.

Shapiro, Edward R., and A. Wesley Carr. *Lost in Familiar Places: Creating New Connections Between the Individual and Society.* New Haven and London: Yale University Press, 1991.

Sheridan, Alan. *Michael Foucault: The Will to Truth*. London: Tavistock Publications, 1980.

Shusaku, Endo. *Deep River*. New York: New Directions, 1994.

Shwender, Richard A. *Thinking Through Cultures: Expeditions in Cultural Psychology*. Cambridge: Harvard University Press, 1991.

Smith, Archie, Jr. "Black Liberation and Process Theologies: Implications for the Care of Black Families." In *Process Studies* 16, no. 1 (spring 1987): 174–90.

———. "The Meaning of Spirituality in the Preparation for Life: An Empirical Approach." *Religious Factors in a Student's Maturing. Focus on Higher Education*. A Colloquium. Santa Barbara, Calif.: Educational Futures, International. March 9–12 (1978): 43–50.

———. *The Relational Self: Ethics and Therapy from a Black Church Perspective*. Nashville: Abingdon Press, 1982.

———. "Religion and Mental Health Among Blacks." *Journal of Religion and Health* 20 (1981): 264–87.

Smith, Daniel L. *The Religion of the Landless: The Social Context of the Babylonian Exile*. Bloomington, Ind.: Meyer-Stone Books, 1989.

Smith, Theophus H. *Conjuring Culture: Biblical Formations of Black America*. New York: Oxford University Press, 1994.

Snyder, Maryhelen, "Becoming: A Method for Expanding Systemic Thinking and Deepening Empathic Accuracy." *Family Process* 34 (1995): 241–52.

Soyinka, Wole. *Myth, Literature and the African World*. Cambridge: Cambridge University Press, 1976.

Spock, Ross V., and Carolyn L. Attneave. *Family Networks: A New Approach to Family Problems*. New York: Vintage Books, 1973.

Still, William. *The Underground Railroad*. Chicago: Johnson Publishing Company, 1970.

Sue, Deral Wing, and David Sue. *Counseling the Culturally Different: Theory and Practice*. 2d ed. New York: John Wiley and Sons, 1990.

Swimme, Brian, and Thomas Berry. *The Universe Story: From the Primordial Flaring Forth to the Ecozoic Era, A Celebration of the Unfolding of the Cosmos*. San Francisco: HarperSanFrancisco, 1992).

Takaki, Ronald. *A Different Mirror: A History of Multicultural America*. Boston: Little, Brown and Company, 1993.

Taylor, Charles. *Human Agency and Language: Philosophical Papers 1*. New York: Cambridge University Press, 1985.

Taylor, Robert Joseph, et al. "Developments in Research on Black Families: A Decade Review." *Journal of Marriage and the Family* 52 (1990): 993–1014.

Tomm, Karl. "Interventive Interviewing: Part I, Strategizing as a Fourth Guideline for the Therapist." *Family Process* 26 (1987): 3–13.

———. "Interventive Interviewing: Part II, Reflexive Questioning as a Means to Enable Self-Healing." *Family Process* 26 (1987): 167–83.

Tomm, Karl, and John Lannamann. "Questions as Interventions." *Networker*, September/October 1988: 38–41.

Turner, Victor. *Dramas, Fields, and Metaphors: Symbolic Action in Human Society*. Ithaca: Cornell University Press, 1974.

Vale, Steiner K., ed. *Psychology and Postmodernism*. London: Sage Publication, 1991.

Watzlawick, Paul. *The Language of Change: Elements of Therapeutic Communication*. New York: Basic Books, 1978.

Weems, Renita J., *Just a Sister Away: A Womanist Vision of Women's Relationships in the Bible*. San Diego: Lura Media, 1988.

West, Cornel. *Keeping Faith: Philosophy and Race in America*. New York: Routledge, 1993.

———. *Race Matters*. Boston: Beacon Press, 1993.

White, Michael. "The Process of Questioning: A Therapy of Literary Merit?" *Dulwich Centre Newsletter*, 1988: 8–14.

Wilson, William Julius. *The Truly Disadvantaged: The Inner City, the Underclass, and Public Policy*. Chicago: University of Chicago Press, 1987.

———. *When Work Disappears: The World of the New Urban Poor*. New York: Alfred A. Knopf, 1996.

Wimberly, Edward Paul. *African American Pastoral Care*, Nashville: Abingdon Press, 1991.

———. *Pastoral Care in the Black Church*. Nashville: Abingdon Press, 1979.

———. *Pastoral Counseling and Spiritual Values: A Black Point of View*, Nashville: Abingdon, 1982.

———. *Prayer in Pastoral Counseling: Suffering, Healing and Discernment*. Louisville, Ky.: Westminster/John Knox Press, 1990.

Wimberly, Edward Paul, and Anne Streaty Wimberly. *Liberation and Human Wholeness: The Conversion Experiences of Black People in Slavery and Freedom*. Nashville: Abingdon Press, 1986.

Winter, Gibson. *Liberating Creation: Foundations of Religious Social Ethics*. New York: Crossroads, 1981.

Winter, Miriam Therese, Adair Lummis, and Allison Stokes. *Defecting in Place: Women Claiming Responsibility for Their Own Spiritual Lives*. New York: Crossroads, 1994.

Woodson, Carter G. *The Mis-Education of the Negro*. Trenton, N.J.: Africa World Press, 1993.

Wright, A. Richard, ed. *African Philosophy: An Introduction*. 3d ed. Lanham, Md.: University Press of America, 1984.

Yarte Kwei Lartey, Emmanuel. *Pastoral Counselling in Inter-Cultural Perspective*. Frankfurt am Main: Verlag Peter Lang, 1987.

Young, Henry James. *Hope in Progress: A Therapy of Social Pluralism*. Minneapolis: Fortress Press, 1990.

Yurugu, Marimba Ani. *An African-Centered Critique of European Cultural Thought and Behaviour*. Trenton, N.J.: Africa World Press, 1994.

INDEX